Dr John Coleman

DRUG WAR AGAINST AMERICA

ℴMNIA VERITAS®

John Coleman

John Coleman is a British author and former member of the Secret Intelligence Service. Coleman has produced various analyses of the Club of Rome, the Giorgio Cini Foundation, Forbes Global 2000, the Interreligious Peace Colloquium, the Tavistock Institute, the Black Nobility and other organisations with New World Order themes.

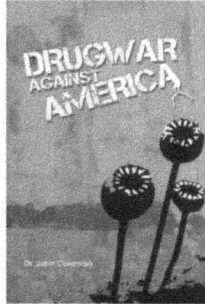

Drug War Against America

© Omnia Veritas Ltd – 2023

OMNIA VERITAS.

www.omnia-veritas.com

Chapter One

Drug War Against America

The first step in solving a problem is to recognize it as such. America has a drug problem, an enormous drug problem that refuses to go away; one that will not be solved until the nation gets to grips with its origin.

The majority of Americans know that there is a drug epidemic, but only a small minority is aware that it was inflicted upon our society by the "rulers of darkness, the wicked men in high places, who prefer darkness rather than light because their deeds are evil."

Who these men are and how they run the largest and most profitable business in the world; what they have achieved and whether there are any effective countermeasures being taken, is the subject matter of this book.

Please do not think that the drug trade is a mere street corner business, where pushers are controlled by the Mafia. Certainly it is part of the problem, but the real promoters of this accursed business are to be found in the halls of the "elite" of this world, the "royal" families, the "noble" families of Europe and the "best" families of America, Britain and Canada. The trade reaches into the highest echelons of power and has not been eradicated, but only somewhat contained. The U.S. Drug Enforcement Agency

(USDA) and drug enforcement agencies around the world are trying to fight a forest fire with garden hoses lacking adequate water-pressure. How can this be?

The answer is that the drug trade cannot be stamped out because its directors, the rulers of darkness, the wicked people in high places, will not allow the most lucrative trade in the world, with lucrative profits requiring the bare minimum of investment capital, a virtually free product with little production cost, to be taken from them. The only problems the controllers of this massive "corporation" have to deal with are delivery and distribution. As I said in one of my White Papers, surely a nation that could mount a massive mobilization effort and send a huge army overseas to fight and win WWII, can mount a campaign to eradicate the drug trade?

Is the drug trade a more formidable task than was waging war against Germany and Japan in the Second World War? Of course not, America can do it. The problem is that Factor X intervenes as soon as the U.S. Drug Enforcement Agency begins to get on top of the problem and Factor X is the ruling elite, whose massive fortunes come from the drug trade.

This trade had its beginning in 1652 and involved several other countries. Britain's aristocratic "upper-crust" actually ran the lucrative Chinese opium trade and Lord Palmerstone of the British Government actually enunciated it from Parliament.

The immense wealth and power enjoyed by the "old money" families of the British aristocracy — the ruling class — can be traced back directly to that odious and dirty business. As I have often said in my Weekly Intelligence Reports and other works, the long struggle for control over Hong Kong that took place between the British and Chinese governments was not about the actual island land mass itself, but about who shall receive the lion's share of the billions of dollars generated by China's opium trade, which accounts for 64 percent of its foreign exchange earnings. The "noble" families of Britain had always taken the biggest slice of the cake, but now that the Chinese have demanded a greater share, what with the collapse of the British Empire and its might, Britain had no option but to grant the request, which settlement came with a condition. Control of the world-wide trade was to remain in British hands, the stained hands of the "noble" and highly-respected "old" families, those who would not give the likes of the American people the time of day, the oligarchy who sit in the seats of power in high places! The drug war against America took a new and ominous turn in the early 1950's, with the introduction of the drug LSD to the youth of America by Aldous Huxley and Bertrand Russell.

LSD is manufactured by the Swiss Oligarchy-Black Nobility family, Hoffman LaRoche. The experiment with LSD was officially under the control of the Stanford Research Center, where extensive experiments were carried out under codenames "Operation Naomi" and "Operation Artichoke" using marijuana and cocaine.

The youth of America disappeared under a blizzard of white powder produced from crinkled green leaves. Willing and unwilling victims were "tested" at such places as The Addiction Center, Mt. Sinai Hospital and the Boston Psychopathic Hospital, to name two of the most important test centers. With the simultaneous promotion of Theo Adorno's 12-Atonal "music" perfected at Wilton Park, home of British propaganda and a center for disinformation, came a stupendous fraud called "rock music" performed by rock bands, which was a medium for the introduction of notorious brainwashing and the drug "testing" programs

The first of a long line of such deceptions was the "discovery" by Ed Sullivan of the drug sodden group "The Beatles." The whole "rock" business was designed and perfected at Wilton Park with the calculated purpose of using it as a vehicle to induce widespread usage of drugs by American youth and make it an acceptable social custom. Rock was planned solely as a vehicle for the spread of drugs and all "rock groups" "discovered" after the Beatles experiment became an integral part of a psychological war waged against the youth of many nations. All the fraudulent groups were put together at Wilton Park by experts who called it "atonal music" after which Wilton Park unleashed a whole series of "rock bands" on an unsuspecting American public. Ed Sullivan, the best known radio personality in the U.S., was complicit in the crime of the century by bringing the "Beatles" to America!

Those taking part in the promotion of rock concerts or distributing records and tapes of the hideously jarring sound, a cacophony of mind-searing noise, should have been prosecuted for their involvement in the spread of drugs. I believe, all "rock" concerts are a criminal offense, because they are used to induce widespread drug usage among the youth. Thus it was that rock concerts were held primarily as a cover for drug distribution and rock "music" became an integral part of the drug war against America. It is time that we, the people, took the gloves off and knocked a few heads together!

It will be doubly-difficult to eradicate the drug trade until "rock music" is eradicated and so called "rock conceits" are outlawed. That means closing down RCA records division and, as those of you who have been following my reports through the years, know that the RCA is an arm of British Intelligence, which began in 1924, when U.S. Marconi was a wholly-owned subsidiary of British Marconi. Then, as now, RCA was run by the British by virtue of control exercised by Morgan Guarantee over the parent group, Westinghouse and General Electric Company. United Fruit Company — now United Brands - whose chairman, Max Fisher, donated huge sums of money to the Republican Party in 1972, held the franchise for all communication equipment sold in Latin America and the Caribbean by the RCA-Westinghouse-G.E. group. United Brands is heavily implicated in the drug trade, as the rare seizure of one of its vessels carrying a large cargo of drugs demonstrated. RCA had ties to Germany before the Second World War, through RCA's chairman David Sarnhoff s lifelong friendship with Hjalmar Schacht, the financial genius behind Hitler. It was friendships of this caliber that prevented "Judge" Jackson from securing a conviction against Schacht at the illegal Nuremberg "trials." Judge Jackson was not a judge at all, but a lawyer, who accepted the U.S. Government's desperate call to fill the vacancy at the Nuremberg trial. The regular judges in the U.S. did not recognize the lawfulness of the Nuremberg proceedings and shunned offers by the Justice Department to represent the U.S. Government.

Let me hasten to add that illegal "recreational" drugs were completely stamped out in Germany while Hitler was in power. RCA, through Sarnhoff (a long time British Intelligence agent), made personal fundraising efforts for various drug-related experiments and projects carried out by Stanford Research Institute, the same institution that oversaw the notorious MK Ultra LSD experimental program.

What about the present? As we reach mid-2009, the overall picture looks very bleak. DEA and international anti-drug authorities have not been able to make even a small dent in the well-protected drug trade infrastructure. In spite of increased efforts by the U.S. DEA, the flood of drugs entering America continues to rise, and is now officially out of control. This is not to say that America cannot stop the trade. What it tells us is that America is fighting a war on drugs with both hands tied behind its back. Efforts to fight the drug menace have the air of a comedy theater production, and will not be any more successful than their previously unsuccessful ventures, unless and until we get at the top people behind the whole drug scene.

The following steps that have not been taken must be taken without any further delay:

➤ Shut-off the spigot of "Foreign Aid" to countries producing the raw materials of the trade.

➤ The U.S. must also enter into a special extradition treaty with drug-producing countries, which would permit DEA agents to operate in producer countries with powers to extradite to the U.S. leading drug producers.

If we were capable of formulating the Nuremberg Statutes for "crimes against humanity," then we must also be capable of an international agreement that would give U.S. agents wide latitude, for is not the drug trade a crime against humanity?

➤ The U.S. must appoint special prosecutors (as we

did in the Tavistock-planned Watergate Conspiracy) to coordinate all drug-related criminal prosecutions.

Inasmuch as the U.S. could establish an international tribunal at Nuremberg, then we most certainly can do the same thing now, since drugs and the whole drug trade is a war against the civilized world - and most definitely a crime against human rights.

> The U.S. must embark on a program to encourage countries producing the raw materials for the trade to sell the entire "crop" to U.S. appointed and controlled officials in concord with a written agreement that no further "crops" be produced.

> U.S. agents must have an agreement that permits the soil in entire grower-areas (like Helmand in Afghanistan, home of the opium poppy) to be rendered unusable to plant poppies.

This can be done and it is a lot cheaper than the enormous cost of policing our coastline and paying the medical bills for victims of the drug trade.

> A step the U.S. can easily take is to pass laws instituting the death penalty for all those caught trafficking, dealing and or pushing drugs.

> Addicts caught smoking or ingesting dope should be tried by a special court and if found guilty, sent to a correction camp in the middle of the Mojave desert with the minimum of human comforts.

There would be a period of amnesty during which all drug dealers must turn in their stocks of drugs to government agencies or specially selected citizen committees, for instant incineration. Thereafter, anyone caught selling drugs or having possession of drugs for sale would be executed.

> ➤ All establishments where drugs are used extensively, such as discos and nightclubs, must be forced to close down — the owners heavily fined and jailed if it is proved in courts of the special prosecutors that drugs were being used on the premises. "Rock concerts" must be outlawed and promoters of rock "concerts" must be heavily fined and jailed.

> ➤ Anyone transporting drugs into the U.S. or across state lines must be tried by the special prosecutors at courts set up for the purpose. Upon a guilty verdict, the traffickers must be sentenced to death and the sentence carried out without undue delay.

> ➤ The U.S. Agricultural Department must make treaties with all drug plant growing countries that will permit teams of U.S. agents to "search and destroy" all places where drug plants are discovered.

This can be done cheaply and effectively be the application of a newly discovered "sunlight killer herbicide" which consists of a compound containing amino acid found in all plants. The compound is harmless to animal life, and overwhelms unwanted growth by a build-up of amino acid in the drug plant, which collapses plant tissue and dehydrates it within three hours.

This new herbicide is capable of wiping out every coca bush, poppy and marijuana field at the source, without any damage to regular crops or poisoning of the soil. Dr. William Robertson of the National Science Foundation said the herbicide is sprayed on just as evening sets in. As soon as the sun rises the next morning, a chain-reaction is triggered and the drug plants begin to "bleed to death" losing all their internal fluids. In a matter of hours, sprayed plants will shrivel up and die. The herbicide is easy to apply, and is inexpensive and environmentally safe. It does not react on food crops such as wheat, barley, oats, soybeans, etc.

With internal support and international agreements, the U.S. could wipe drugs off the face of the earth within a matter of three years and at an amazingly low cost. The program can become operational through treaties and concordats. Any country refusing to join the program, which would include a clause mandating U.S. agents to be stationed in them, would have all U.S. foreign aid funding cut off.

A world-wide trade boycott (as was enforced against Germany in 1933) must be instituted against those countries refusing to sign and international pressures brought to bear upon them through all United Nation agencies, of the kind that was ruthlessly applied against South Africa and Iraq. The new product, ALA, is already available and the U.S. must embark upon a crash program to produce it in sufficient quantities for use on a global scale.

We must mobilize for war! To implement this program in its entirety will require concentrated effort, but no bigger than it took in 1939-45. If we could make the mighty effort of the Second World War, then we are obligated to make the same effort now. America's security was never directly threatened by Germany in 1939. Germany had no quarrel with the U.S., but the Drug Merchants, the "noble families," do pose a direct and very present dangerous threat to our security and future well- being as a great nation. The U.S. must declare war against such countries and their bases of production and their transportation and distribution systems must be wiped out. We must mobilize our massive resources in human and technical potential to meet the Drug Lords and destroy them.

For the past 34 years, the American people have watched helplessly as the tide of war went against them. Up to now the American people did not realize that we are at war because the enemy could not be as readily identified as our propaganda mills identified Germany in 1939. Those same propaganda "opinion makers" are very reluctant to tackle the Drug Merchants, which is not at all surprising when one realizes that the "opinion makers" are a part of the same network. There is a grave need to bring home to Americans that the obscene profits from drugs that ruin millions of lives each year, also fund international terrorism.

Recent DEA statistics show an alarming increase in the number of users of heroin, cocaine and marijuana in America. As for the terrorist aspect, one has only recall the activities of the "Shining Pathway" cult sect in Peru to see how drug money funded murder.

This group was one of the most violent and vicious terrorist gangs in the world, a gang of thugs bent on taking over Peru in order to get control of the lucrative cocaine business, until President Fujimoro of Peru got personally involved. But it was a move that was to cost him his presidency and his having to flee to Japan in fear of his life.

Cocaine is an increasing menace which affects 20 million Americans. Made popular by the "smart set" and the Hollywood "in-crowd," it is attracting an estimated 5,000 new users each day! Frank Monastero of the DEA stated recently that links to terrorism through the drug trade are very strong, "but I do not think it is being looked at in that way by certain segments in the administration." Although Monastero did not say to which "segment" he was referring, I know from conversations I've had with certain U.S. officials that he was talking about the U.S. State Department.

The State Department has consistently voiced its opposition to linking drug enforcement methods to suspension of "Foreign Aid" and has disagreed with implementing methods I've outlined in this book. It is a well-known fact that State Department officials consider a narcotics control appointment abroad as the least desirable foreign service posting.

The Royal Institute for International Affairs (RIIA) and Council on Foreign Relations (CFR), who control the Rand Corporation (the organization that gave us Daniel Ellsberg of the Pentagon Papers notoriety), made matters worse by writing an unsolicited paper, which claimed that efforts to combat drug usage on the educational level "are conflicting, ambiguous and have zero effect." This is palpably untrue, but what else can we expect from an institution run by The Tavistock Institute of Human Relations whose masters are the very ones who profit from the vile drug trade? The Rand report was like firing on our own troops, for if it had fired on the drug crowd, it would have been firing on its friends, not its enemies! The net result of the Rand report has been to discourage anti-drug educational programs. Yet, Rand receives large grants from the U.S. government — an example of contradictions in our efforts to minimize the drug trade.

The General Accounting Office (GAO) estimates that only ten percent of drugs smuggled into America get intercepted by law enforcement agencies. This ought to set the alarm bells ringing! How is it that a highly industrialized nation with such large manpower, money and technical resources is only able to intercept such a small percentage of the drugs? We must look for the "hidden hand," the power controlling the drug trade from behind the scenes, the mysterious "Force X." To get the proper answer to the question I will deal with that aspect as we proceed.

A document of recent date that I have seen states that the production of opium poppies in China has increased by 50 percent since 2000. Other statistics in the document mentioned above show that marijuana and coca leaf production has increased by 30 and 40 percent, and opium production from poppies in Afghanistan has risen from 4,000lbs. to 6,000 lbs. a year since the invasion of that country by U.S. and NATO troops in 2003. How has this feat been accomplished? It has been accomplished by an all-out war against America directed by the RIIA, Wilton Park, the Tavistock Institute and the CFR and the ruling oligarchy the Black Nobility families of Europe. Their chief tool in this war has been ~ and still is — "rock groups" and "rock concerts" and the ceaseless promotion of the decadent 12-atonal cacophony of mind-destroying sound that passes for "music." This tool was first used in 1950 and is the principal weapon in the enemy arsenal in its war on America and will continue to be used to spread drugs until someone puts an end to it once and for all!

Getting back to the heroin business, the main poppy

growing locations are found in the so-called "Golden Triangle" of Southeast Asia and the "Golden Crescent" in Iran, Afghanistan and Pakistan, respectively.

It is as well to remember the British "Blue Blood" families made their fortunes out of shipping opium from the fields of Afghanistan and Pakistan to users in China, in which countries they built for a 100 years, the necessary contacts that enabled them to safely and profitably carry on the trade today.

As for the Middle East, the bulk of raw opium transits through Lebanon, Syria and Turkey. After an interim processing, it travels to Europe via Frankfort. The so-called "Frankfort Mafia" runs the distribution end of the business, and the notorious Meyer Lanskey (a leading member of the Crime Syndicate, now deceased) was the kingpin in that operation. Upon Lanskey's death, the position passed to Israeli General Ariel Sharon, which he held up to his unlamented departure. Sharon had very strong ties with "grower" countries such as Bolivia and Peru, both major producers of the coca leaf from which cocaine is derived. Lebanon was invaded so that the country could be split up into fiefdoms, and, as I disclosed in one of my reports, Rifaad Assad, brother of Syrian President Hafez Assad, was first placed under house arrest and then banished from Syria because of the "private" deals he was making with Sharon. Rifaad Assad's expulsion from Syria became a matter of public record, but the real reason behind it — drug related infractions — was never made public.

Secret Senate reports indicate that the U.S. State Department did not follow President Reagan's directive that drug grower countries must be reprimanded. This should not come as a surprise, given the background and control exercised by Chatham House through British operative George Shultz, the former Secretary of State appointed by President G.H.W. Bush, a former titular head of the Eastern Liberal Establishment who has very strong ties to the drug trade.

Drug producing countries hold the position that the drug problem is an American one, and as long as there is an American demand for drugs, producer-countries are only fulfilling that demand. This view entirely overlooks the fact that in China, originally, there was no demand for opium, up to and until it was "created" by the same unscrupulous "noble" families who then met the "need" and supplied the opium. It also overlooks the fact that the same families are still running the trade, but this time the recipient country is the U.S. Some Senators hold the view that the way to halt the trade is to "legalize" drugs, starting with marijuana and cocaine. Of course, they are quick to add that it should be small amounts for private use only.

This is tantamount to fighting a fire by pouring gasoline on it! The same people put private armies in position in Peru, Bolivia and Colombia to protect their enormous investments in the drug trade in these countries. Senator Paula Hawkins of Florida has confirmed this, as have private sources of information, which obviously cannot be named. In Bolivia, Colombia and Peru, these well-armed private armies have fought pitched battles with government troops and often defeated them!

As a result, the bandits now have complete control in the "growing" areas and government officials have to obtain permission to enter such areas! Naturally, permission is never given and government agents entering the "exclusion zone" do so at the risk of being murdered, as indeed many are. Senator Hawkins was all for shutting down "foreign aid" to offending countries and announced her intention of so doing. Senator Hawkins was chairman of the Senate Committee on Alcohol and Drug abuse, but soon lost her job once she became too insistent. Hawkins faced very strong opposition from within the State Department, as "foreign aid" is what they think of as strictly their province, not to be interfered with. Since 1946, when David Rockefeller instituted this insidious give-away of U.S. taxpayer money and the CFR got it on the law books, the State Department has taken a "hands-off" attitude with regard to the foreign aid swindle. Former acting Assistant Secretary of State for narcotics, Clyde D. Taylor, put the State Department's position as follows:

> We have to keep the drug problem in perspective — we have other diplomatic interests in these countries, and if we go in and alienate them over drugs, we may be sorry when we need them a few years later for something else. The idea of revoking foreign aid is not as simple as it may seem. We don't have as much clout as you might think.

What an admission!

Nevertheless, notwithstanding opposition from the British-controlled State Department, some progress, at least on paper, has been made during the last five years. Drug control agreements were negotiated with Pakistan, Bolivia, Peru, Mexico and Columbia although on very narrow grounds.

With regard to Pakistan, the largest trade route for raw opium in the world, it is doubtful whether the agreement will have any effect on the flow of opium into America, because military leaders and other law enforcement agencies oppose any real control. Ali Bhutto, the former President of Pakistan, was the only one who actively opposed the drug trade under the protection of the military and was judicially murdered by General Zia ul Haq who succeeded him. Bhutto was fully committed to stamping out the drug trade in Pakistan, and his strong stand against drugs no doubt led to his death. So don't expect any slowing down in the Pakistan opium trade. It is being carried on even though the Attorney General William French Smith of the United States went to Pakistan and personally appealed to the government to terminate it with substantial U.S. help. President ul Haq's answer was to warn William French Smith to get out of Pakistan, as he was unable to guarantee his personal safety. Since then no U.S. Attorney General has visited Pakistan.

On the other side of the world, the number one cocaine producer is Colombia, although it appears through a recent discovery of new coca plantations in Brazil, that it is likely to lose its place to Brazil.

Cocaine is classified as "non-habit forming" and several eminent physicians in the pay of the Drug Merchants declared it as having no lasting harmful effects. But all that changed, when a courageous doctor told the New York Times, that tests conducted with cocaine show that over the long haul, users suffer severe brain damage. According to DEA statistics I have seen, 75 percent of all cocaine, and 59 percent of all marijuana reaching American originates in Colombia.

Bolivia produces 10%, as does Peru, with Mexico producing 9 percent of the marijuana. Locally grown marijuana accounts for 11 percent of the market, with 9% from Jamaica.

Cocaine "manufacture" is a relatively simple process. The plant from which the leaf is taken grows wild, but nowadays, it is also cultivated in plantations. The leaves are stripped from the bush by cheap local peasant labor, placed on tarpaulins and then stamped on, after which kerosene and calcium carbonate are poured on the partly mashed-up leaves, causing a white paste to appear. Sulfuric acid is then added and the mixture is filtered, after which a deadly chemical, acetone, is added and the mixture left to dry. Some add white wine to the mix, which after a suitable time turns into a pure white crystalline powder -cocaine. It takes about 300 pounds of coca leaves to produce one pound of cocaine. The cost of labor and raw material is so cheap that profits up to 5,000 percent are usual at the primary producer stage.

The Colombian drug trade was, until recently, fully protected by the military, the judiciary and the banks, but that came to a stop when President Betancourt took office in 1991. Dissident military officers who were accustomed to making big profits from their slice of the cocaine trade, and who were not prepared to support Betancourt's anti-drug program, found themselves stripped of rank and position. But since Betancourt's departure, things have reverted to "normal." Most of the money derived from the trade finds its way into banks in Florida, and Swiss Banks. The Swiss press even went as far as to openly criticize President Betancourt, claiming that his anti-cocaine policy would deal Colombia's economy a severe blow and cost the country dearly in foreign exchange. This is of course a big lie, since most of the "foreign exchange" never goes back to Colombia, finishing up in the vaults of Swiss banks instead. No wonder the Swiss bankers didn't like Betancourt's anti-cocaine stand!

Strongly lined up against Betancourt were elements of the Gnostic Church. In Colombia, the MI9 guerillas (known by their Spanish acronym FARC) deny that most of their income is from drug related sources. Betancourt got the leader, Dr. Carlos Toledo Plata, to sign an agreement with the Colombian government that brought about a truce in the fighting, but it was not very long before Plata was murdered by the Drug Merchants.

Shortly after that murder, two thugs mounted on a motorcycle shot and killed Colombian Justice Minister Rodrigo Lara Bonilla, on the afternoon of April 30, 1984. Both men escaped to the drug capital Santa Marta, where they are protected by the private armies of the FARC revolutionary army. Both murders were looked upon with favor by the Drug Merchants, who have a great deal to lose if Colombia should succeed in stamping out its drug trade. Former President Lopez Michelson was heavily involved in the cocaine trade before he was ousted. He fled to the country following an abortive kidnapping plan of an antidrug deputy and went into hiding in Paris. His cousin Jamie Michelson Urbane keeps a big bankroll in Miami.

Michelson was in deep trouble for suggesting that the Colombian Government negotiate an agreement with the Drug Merchants. Drug-money banker Urbane, once the Chairman of Banco de Colombia, before fleeing to Miami on the same day two of his managers were arrested by Betancourt under Decree Number 2920. The order for the military to begin spraying all fields where drug plants were growing with paraquat (a chemical agent that defoliates plants and bushes) was a major blow to the Drug Merchant barons, and those who stood to benefit the most from cocaine money, the oligarchs of the Black Nobility of Europe.

Betancourt, by demonstrating his intent to crush the drug trade, was no mere rhetoric and faced a grave threat of assassination. Nobody should believe that the Drug Barons and Europe's Blue Bloods would take attacks on their trade lying down.

I well recall that when American officials approached British officials in a highly secret meeting held in Cambridge, England in 1985 to ask for help in combating the drug trade in the Bahamas, they were refused help or information. This will not surprise anyone knowing the Bahamas, where the whole government is in the drug business run out of certain Masonic lodges in England, and proceeds are laundered through the Royal Bank of Canada. (Remember Canada is only an outpost of the British Royal Family and not a country in the same sense that America is a country.)

Some of the leading American banks in such places as Panama, facilitate the flow of money - presently estimated at $550 million per year — acting as convenient channels for top people in Britain, Canada and the U.S. It will be recalled that General Manuel Noriega came to grief when he ripped the lid off one of the Rockefeller banks in Panama engaged in drug money laundering, in the mistaken belief that he was carrying out the wishes of the U.S. DEA. It is not only banks that protect and shield the lucrative trade. The International Monetary Fund (IMF) plays an ever increasingly important role in the trade. There is a great deal of evidence on hand showing that the IMF has been protecting the drug trade since 1960, but particularly with regard to top British institutions and the "noble" families running them.

In England, it is perfectly legal to use drugs, but not to

market them. This is in keeping with IMF policies and as far as Colombia is concerned, takes the position that Colombia has the right to earn foreign currency by exporting narcotics to wherever the demand is. This is on the grounds that income earned by narcotics helps to repay IMF loans - which are absolutely false. The Central Banking Department of the IMF works exclusively with offshore banks that receive large cash deposits from the drug trade.

After the brutal and blatant murder of Columbia's Justice Minister, Rodrigo Lara Bonilla, IMF and Club of Rome "connections" panicked and began to distance themselves from M19 drug trade "troops," because Betancourt angrily mobilized all available reserves, calling the murder a "blight on Colombia's name." Going directly to the public, Betancourt called upon all citizens to help him in his struggle against the traffickers, saying "national dignity is held hostage by these traffickers."

The Catholic Church was asked to join in the struggle, and agreed to throw its weight behind the President, with only the Order of the Jesuits standing aloof. President Reagan would have done well to emulate Betancourt's tactics, and I believe he would have received such a mighty outpouring of support from the people as has never been witnessed. But, sadly, Reagan did not do so. It is gratifying to note that although the Jesuits and the Gnostics joined forces with the M19 guerillas to disrupt

Betancourt's anti-drug efforts, they made only slight headway, notwithstanding the powerful "hidden-hand" supporting their combined disruptive tactics. Betancourt granted DEA the right to come into Colombia and spray drug plants with paraquat. He has also granted several extradition requests for top Colombian drug traffickers the U.S. has long sought to get its hands on. But the U.S. has thus far failed to reciprocate and failed to return Michelson Urbane to Colombia.

During her visit to Colombia, Senator Hawkins praised the Colombian President's determined efforts to uproot the Drug Merchants. But my sources told me that in spite of a noticeable slowing down of cocaine to America, evidenced by a sharp increase in its price that does not mean the drug overlords are not fighting back. There is evidence that they have extended their activities in Argentina and Brazil to secure new plantation sites for coca bushes.

Some Colombian officials, not wholly committed to President Betancourt, claimed they could not penetrate remote jungle sites where the traffickers were operating. The question is, if the drug traffickers can get in there, why can't government anti-drug forces do likewise? There is an urgent need to attack these plantation sites because evidence has come to light showing experimental fields of opium poppies (from which heroin is derived) growing in these remote "impenetrable" regions, according to John T. Cassack of the House Select Committee on Narcotics Abuse and Control. "Los grandes mafioses" have come a long way since 1970 when they really began to get cocaine sales in the U.S. moving. In 2006, they began to use fleets of boats, planes, helicopters and a heavily armed private army. They were careful to act as public benefactors, financing many public projects. The public sees them as "smart operators" taking advantage of a purely U.S. problem, an insatiable American demand for cocaine and marijuana. One of the overlords, Pablo Escobar Gavira, poured huge sums of money into slum improvements, a program administered by the Jesuits who always favored the immensely wealthy Gavira.

Gavira once spent $50,000 on his daughter's wedding and got himself elected as a parliamentary deputy, thus obtaining parliamentary immunity from arrest. He was wanted by the U.S. DEA authorities for years. But after Justice Minister Lara was cut down by 22 bullets from an Uzi submachine gun, a great revulsion swept over the Colombian people. They turned on "los grandes mafioses" and things began to happen. Even the Jesuits distanced themselves from Gavira. With jurisdiction in drug related cases turned over to the military, the many judges who used to attend lavish parties given by the drug merchants, were stripped of their former power. Bishop Dario Castrillon also tried to deny his connection with Drug merchants, saying the money he received from them was to build churches. Bribing judges was no longer acceptable, and the military courts established to try drug cases could not be reached by the bribers.

Even the powerful Ochoa family ran for cover, but even their man, President Lopez Michelson, was in trouble. Ochoa called him in Panama, where he was consulting with other top drug traffickers, to warn him about the wholesale arrests going on at home. Incidentally, Gavira and the three Ochoa brothers representing 100 of the top drug dealers went to Michelson for help, but he failed them. However, the gangsters were not finished. In an astonishing development, the Ochoas met with Colombian Attorney General Carlos Jimenez Gomez in Panama. For some reason, Gomez failed to notify U.S. authorities about the meeting. Had he done so, the U.S. DEA agents would have reaped a rich harvest of arrests in Panama! The U.S. Ambassador, Alexander Watson, wasn't informed of the meeting by Gomez until two months after the event. This brings up another question. Since it is known that U.S. drug enforcement agents closely shadow all the leading Colombian Drug Merchants, how is it possible that these agents were unaware of the meeting in Panama? The hidden hand, the powerful families of America and Europe, the Swiss bankers, the IMF and Club of Rome, P2 Masons and probably the CFR, appear to have intervened at this point.

The Ochoas delivered a 72-page memo to the Attorney General, offering to dismantle the entire cocaine operation in Colombia in exchange for being allowed to return to Colombia without fear of arrest. The memo was delivered to U.S. authorities who replied that they did not make deals with criminals. As for Attorney General Gomez, his flimsy excuse for meeting with the drug overlords and failing to inform his government thereof in advance was that he went to Panama on other business (which he neglected to specify) and quite by accident met the Ochoas. Gomez did not explain why he did not immediately telephone President Betancourt and inform him of the development. The truth is that Gomez was acting on orders from the "hidden hand" in the Colombia drug cartel. In Colombia, the Attorney General is appointed by their Congress and is not required to answer to the President. But many Congressmen were deeply angered by Gomez's strange actions and called for his resignation, which he declined.

Escobar Gavira began operating out of Nicaragua under the protection of Jesuit priests in the Sandinista government. Secretly taken photographs showed Gavira and his men loading cocaine onto a plane in that country appeared to me to be quite genuine, but were undated. Was this an indication that the Jesuit dominated Nicaraguan Government of the period had joined in the drug war against America? Yet the majority of House and Senate members consistently refused to grant President Reagan the authority he needed to topple the Sandinista government.

> The question is why do "our" representatives oppose every effort to get rid of the Jesuit-Communist Nicaraguan Government?

> More than that, why did so many of them vote in favor of "foreign aid" and "loans" for Nicaragua?

> Why did Senators de Concini and Richard Lugar vote to give the Communist Sandinistas our tax money?

> Why support people like Manuel de Escoto, who was reputed not only helps drug traffickers get their dangerous cargoes into America, but went around the world attacking America on every possible occasion?

Until the power of the hidden hand, the Club of Rome-CFR-Trilateral Eastern Establishment and their allies in high places are exposed, America cannot and will not win this terrible war. All our efforts will come to naught. Until the U.S. Government prevails upon Panama to stop the huge imports of what I call drug chemicals, the cocaine trade in Colombia will not be stamped out.

What does Panama want with enormous quantities of kerosene, ether and acetone? These chemicals, as everybody knows, are not allowed as direct imports into Colombia, so it is obvious that Panama's imports are transshipped indirectly and illegally into Colombia.

After this was written in 2003, Columbia has been forced deeper and deeper into becoming an all out drug state. The guerillas have become a great deal better organized, thanks to three factors:

> The take over of Panama, which has resulted in a 65% increase in drugs flowing into the Panama Canal area.

> Easy money laundering by Panama's banks.

> Increased support for the MI9 guerillas provided by Castro.

This has resulted in better quality arms now reaching the MI9 in larger quantities, coupled with increased cash reserves, all making for an expanded drug trade in Columbia. Pablo Escobar was "arrested" in a highly publicized raid on his luxury home and compound, but recent intelligence reports claims that after a short stay in an American prison, he was spirited out of the U.S. Present whereabouts said to be "unknown."

When I was doing research through my hundreds of shorthand notebooks on this vital subject, I came across some interesting statistics I had noted in my investigative work in London. It deals with the fact that in 1930, British capital invested in South America greatly exceeded its total investment in the so called "dominions." On November 30, a certain Mr. Graham, an authority on the subject, said that British investment in South America "exceeded one trillion pounds." Now this was back in 1930, and in those days it was a staggering sum of money. What was the reason why the British invested so heavily in South America? The answer adds up to one word: DRUGS.

The plutocracy controlling British banks held the purse strings, and then as now, put up the most respectable facade.

No one ever caught them with their hands dirtied; they always had front men and willing stooges ready and waiting up front to take the blame. Then as now, the connections are always of the most tenuous kind. No one could ever lay a finger on the respectable "noble" banking families of Britain, not then, and not today. But there is a great significance in the fact, that 15 members of Parliament were the controllers of this vast empire in South America, including the Chamberlain family and the family of Sir Charles Barry.

The overlords of British finance and respectability, always crowing about oppression in South Africa where the blacks have the best conditions in all of Africa, were also very busy in places like Trinidad and Jamaica, where they also held the reins in the drug business. In these countries, the plutocrats of the respectable families of British aristocracy kept the blacks at a level barely above that of slavery, while paying themselves a handsome dividend. Of course they hid behind respectable companies like Trinidad Leaseholds Ltd. (an oil company), but the real meat was and still is, in the drug trade.

Up to a short while ago, the opium trade in China was not a well-known subject. It had been as well covered up, as it was possible to do. Many of my students used to come to me and ask why the Chinese were so fond of opium. They were puzzled about contradictory accounts of what had actually taken place in China. Some thought that it was simply a case of the Chinese workingman buying opium locally and smoking it in some opium den. I did my best to enlighten those enquiring minds.

The truth is that the opium trade in China was a British Monopoly subject to official British policy. The Indo-

British opium trade to China is one of the most carefully kept secrets and one of the most dastardly chapters in the history of European colonialism. Statistics show that almost 13 percent of the income of India under British rule was derived from the sale of opium to Chinese addicts. The addicts just did not appear out of thin air; they were created. That is to say, a market for opium was first created among the Chinese and then the "demand" was filled by the British oligarchy, the overlords of the various banking houses of London. This lucrative trade is one of the worst examples of making money out of human misery, and provides a unique record of the dirty business deals conducted by the City of London, which still today, remains the center of "dirty deals" in the financial world. Of course you will doubt the statement, "look at the Financial Times" you say, "it is filled with legitimate business deals." Of course it is, but you don't think that the noble aristocrats are going to advertise the true source of their income in the Financial Times, do you?

The British did not advertise the fact that the opium was shipped from the Benares and Ganges valleys in India to China, where it was partially-processed under a state administered monopoly, an administration which existed solely to oversee the opium trade. You would not have expected to have read that in the London Times of the period, would you?

Yet this trade has been conducted since 1652 by the illustrious East India Company, on whose board of directors sat the holiest of holy of the British aristocracy. They were a species above the common herd of mankind. They were so high and mighty they believed even God came to them for advice when He had a problem in Heaven! Later the British Crown joined this scurrilous East India Company and used it as a vehicle to produce opium in Bengal and elsewhere in India and control exports through what it called "transit duties," that is to say, a tax levied on all producers of opium, duly registered with the state authority, who were sending their output to China. Prior to 1885 when it was still "illegal" (this was merely a word used to exact greater tribute from the producers of opium - there was never any attempt to stop the trade) absolutely colossal amounts of opium were shipped out to China. So audacious had the British become, that far away, on the other side of the world, the British tried to sell the Union and Confederate Armies this lethal substance in pill form. Can you imagine what would have become of America if the plan had succeeded? Every soldier who survived that terrible tragedy would have left the battlefield, completely hooked on opium.

The Bengal merchants and bankers grew fat and contented on the enormous amounts of money that poured into their coffers from this trade of Bengal opium purchased by the British East India Company (BEIC), which is why their profits were in the region of the profits made by the number-one medical drug company, Hoffman La Roche, the same Hoffman La Roche that manufactures LSD among other things. Hoffman La Roche invokes the Swiss Industrial Espionage Act against anyone who dares to expose their rapacious greed, so one has to be careful when expressing an opinion.

In any event, Hoffman La Roche manufactures a commonly used drug called Valium. It costs them around $3.50 per 2.5 pounds. They sell it for $20,000 per kilo, and by the time the American public, which uses Valium in astronomical amounts, gets it, the price is $50,000 per kilo! Hoffman La Roche does much the same thing with Vitamin C, on which it has a similar monopoly. It costs them around 1 cent per kilo to produce and they sell it for a profit, of something like ten thousand percent.

When a brave man by the name of Adams, who once worked for them, disclosed this information to the European Economic Commission's (EEC Monopolies Commission), he was arrested and maltreated by the Swiss police who kept him in solitary confinement for three months. Then he was kicked out of his job and out of Switzerland, losing his pension and everything else. As a British national, he kept fighting Hoffman La Roche. Remember that, the next time you see those oh so correct and polite Swiss businessmen. Switzerland is not just Alpine ski slopes and pristine air under blue skies. Its banking industry has long been suspected of thriving on the drug businesses, legal and illegal, and the enormous profits made by the top men of the drug trade, these hounds from hell. The "clean" image of Switzerland begins to look tarnished when one pulls up the corner of the covers. During her time as Prime Minister, Mrs. Thatcher went on a tour of British Customs posts at Heathrow London airport. Her purpose was to give the Customs officers a "pep talk" on combating the drug menace. What hypocrisy. The leading British conservative newspaper derided Mrs. Thatcher's effort but did not call her a hypocrite, or in any sense divulge the truth about who is behind the menace.

"Oh," you say, "but both the Americans and the British have made some notable drug busts recently." Yes, but that represents 0.0009 percent of the total value of drugs available on the open market. It is what the top drug merchants and their respectable bankers call "part of the cost of doing business." No one who has attended the funeral of a young drug addict — and there are many every day - can fail to be moved by the Prime Minister's remarks about the drug problems facing Britain. No one was likely to baulk at her strictures on pushers. "We are after you," she said. "We will pursue you relentlessly."

Mrs. Thatcher:

> The effort will get greater and greater until we have beaten you. The penalty will be long prison sentences. The penalty will be confiscating everything you have got from drug smuggling. There will also be widespread support among Britons to reject appeals from abroad to help Britons caught smuggling drugs, particularly of a young Briton facing the death sentence in Malaysia for trying to smuggle heroin through Penang airport. There is no point in appealing to us. All over Malaysia you will find posters saying the penalty for dealing in drugs is death.

This is fine, but then it should be applied to all those at the top of the aristocratic heap in England with equal force. When a young Briton was executed in Malaysia for drug smuggling, then so should have been half of those listed in Debretts Peerage (a high society listing of titled English families). Who did Mrs. Thatcher think would be affected by her "tough" new stance? Did she think that the top families in Hong Kong, the Keswicks and the Mathesons, were going to be intimidated by her rhetoric? While her words may have had the effect of frightening a few of the small fry, the big fat sleek fish escaped her drag net and the small fry who were caught, were soon replaced by thousands of others, eager to take their place.

The drug menace will not be countered by fighting it on the street corner level. As far as I am concerned, and in my opinion, based upon my years of research into the subject, the drug business, at least in Britain, is run by the very top people in the British hierarchy, even, making use of such institutions as the Venerable Order of St John of Jerusalem.

As far back as 1931, the managing directors of the so-called Big Five companies in England were rewarded by being made peers of the realm. Who chooses how honors are bestowed upon the leaders of the top echelon in the drug business? In England it is Queen Elizabeth Guelph, better known as the ruling head of the House of Windsor. Banks involved in this trade are too numerous to list, but a few of the main ones are the Midland Bank, the National and Westminster Bank, Barclays Bank and of course, the Royal Bank of Canada.

Many so-called "merchant bankers" in the City of London are up to their eyebrows in the drug trade, venerable financial institutions such as Hambros for example. Let me be more specific and mention such illustrious names as Sir Anthony Eden's family.

According to secret documents I saw, and according to my best analyses of these documents, the Eden family would have qualified for Mrs. Thatcher's "honors list." If one were able to examine the records of the India Office in London as I was fortunate to do, I believe it would become apparent that there is no other conclusion to be drawn. I am deeply indebted to the trustee of the papers of the late Professor Frederick Wells Williamson for the help and assistance given me in my studies of these documents. If the papers were to be made public, what a storm would burst over the heads of the crowned vipers in Europe! The flood of heroin threatens to engulf the Western world. The vast enterprise is run and financed on both sides of the Atlantic — by certain members of the British-U.S. Liberal Establishment.

What is heroin?

It is a derivative of opium, and opium says the noted authority Galen, is a drug that stupefies the senses and induces sleep. It is also one of the most habit forming-dependency drugs on the market. The seed of the poppy, from which opium paste is derived, was long ago known to the Moguls of India, who it is recorded, used poppy seeds mixed with tea leaves and served the brew to their enemies when it was inexpedient to cut off their heads. As far back as 1613, the first opium reached England from Bengal via the East India Company, but such imports were only the smallest amounts. The English yeoman and middle class could not be induced to take the drug, which was the reason why the British East India Company imported it in the first place. With such a signal failure, the oligarchy began to cast around for a market that would not be so unbending, and China was their choice. In the papers The Miscellaneous Old Records of the India Office, I found confirmation that the opium trade really took off with the introduction of the drug into China. This is confirmed also in the personal papers of Sir George Birdwood an official of the British East India Company (BEIC). Vast quantities of opium were soon being shipped to China. Where the BEIC failed in England, it now succeeded beyond its highest projections among the "coolies" in China, whose wretched lives were made bearable by the drug.

It was not until 1729 that the first of many laws against opium smoking were enacted by the Chinese government and from this time on, the British oligarchy entered into a running battle with the Chinese authorities, a battle which the Chinese lost. The U.S authorities are likewise conducting a running battle with today's dope barons, and just as the Chinese lost their battle, so too is the U.S. losing the ongoing battle.

When I talk of Bengal opium from India, I am talking about opium made from seed pods of opium poppies grown in the Ganges Basin. The best opium comes from Bihar and Benares, and of course there is much opium of an inferior quality from other areas of India. Latterly some excellent quality opium (if one can apply the word "excellent" to so dangerous a product) is coming out of Pakistan in very sizeable quantities. The profit from this vast trade was known for many years as "The Spoils of the Empire."

In a noted trial held in 1791, a certain Warren Hastings was put on charges that he had helped enrich a friend at the expense of the East India Company. The actual wording is interesting, because it confirms the enormous amount of money that was being made.

The charge was that Hastings had granted "a contract for the Provision of Opium for four years to Stephen Sullivan Esq. without advertising for the same, on terms glaringly obvious and wantonly profuse, for the purpose of creating an instant fortune for the said Stephen Sullivan Esq." As the semi-official and later official East India Company held the monopoly, the only people allowed to make "instant fortunes" were the so-called "nobility," the "aristocracy," and the oligarchy families of England. Outsiders like Mr. Sullivan, soon found themselves in trouble if they were so bold as to try and help them to get into the multi- billion pound sterling act!

In 1986 I saw a publication from the most dubious source (by this I mean that it was obviously a product of the Third Department of the KGB), that purported to show the drug trade was linked to the mythical "Nazis." The organization that printed the stuff is always after the Nazis. If a camel in the zoo in New York caught a cold, it would be the fault of the mythical "Nazis."

Five years of investigation, including several personal conversations with the man who was allegedly the head and organizing genius behind the mythical Nazi bank accounts in Swiss banks, left me convinced that the authors of the printed material were dragging a red herring over the trail. The so called "Nazis" have nothing whatever to do with the drug trade, unlike the British and the U.S. — a fact very well-known to the U.S. DEA.

As I have noted so many times before, there are still doubters, that the honorable BEIC, with its long list of directors who were honorable Members of Parliament and belonged to only the best gentlemen's clubs in London, carried on the lucrative opium trade and brooked no interference from the British government or anyone else for that matter. Trade between Britain and China was the monopoly of the BEIC. The company had a neat little trick; most of its members in India and at home, were also magistrates. Even passports issued by the company were needed to land in China.

When a number of investigators arrived in China to investigate opium trade allegations being made in England, their British passports were promptly revoked by the East India Company's "magistrates." Friction with the Chinese government was common. Officially, China had passed a law (the Yung Cheng Edict of 1729) prohibiting the importation of opium. Yet the British East India Company saw to it that opium still appeared in the Chinese customs tariff book up until 1753, the duty being three taels per chest of opium. Back then the monarch of England's special secret service (the "007" of the day) saw to it that troublesome people were bought off, or if they could not be bought off because they had plenty of money of their own, they were simply eliminated.

British colonial capitalism has always been the main stay of the oligarchist feudal systems of England, and remains so up until this day. When the poor, untutored and militarily ill-equipped South African farmer-guerillas fell into the drug-stained hands of the British aristocracy in 1899, they had no idea that the relentlessly cruel war waged against them, was made possible only by the incredible amounts of money, which came from the "instant fortunes" of the British drug trade in China, and flowed into the pockets of plutocrats, who engineered the war. The real instigators of the war were Barney Barnato and Alfred Belt, both from Germany, and Cecil John Rhodes, an agent for the Rothschild banking house, a bank awash in a sea of cash generated by the drug trade. Not satisfied, they wanted the riches of the gold and diamonds that lay beneath the barren soil of the South African veld. These three men robbed the Boers, the rightful owners of the gold and diamonds of a stupendous fortune, and in this they were aided and abetted and protected by the British Parliament.

The Joels and the Oppenheimers who were the leading families involved in gold and diamond mining are in my studied opinion, the biggest thieves ever to deface this Earth, and I make no apology whatsoever for making such a harsh judgment.

The average South African, who should have benefited from the billion upon billions of dollars worth of gold and diamonds extracted from beneath the soil of South Africa, received almost nothing from this immense fortune. In short, the South Africans have been robbed blind of their birthright, because unlike true capitalism, the Babylonian capitalist system operating in South Africa does not permit wealth to be shared; it does not filter down to those who have earned it.

This is the crime of the century, financially speaking, and it was all made possible through the vast fortune from the opium trade, which allowed Queen Victoria to finance a great war of oppression against the Boers. It is practically impossible for an outsider to penetrate the secrets of the British oligarchy and the interrelated families that make it up. I estimate that 95 percent of the British population must be content with less than 20 percent of the national wealth of the country, and that is what they call "democracy." No wonder then the Founding Fathers of the American Republic hated and despised "democracy."

The camouflage the oligarchists have painted over themselves as a protective coloring is very hard to penetrate. Nonetheless, it affects the lives of every American, since what Britain dictates, America carries out.

History is replete with such examples. We have only to look at British propaganda that got America into the First World War via the big lie of the sinking of the Lusitania, to see how true my statement is. We are not dealing with "nice, proper British gentlemen" here; we are dealing with ruthless elite who are determined to protect their way of life, and who are inextricably woven and intertwined with the drug business.

The majority of British political leaders of any importance

are all descendants of so called titled families, the title being passed at the death of the holder to the eldest son. This system has camouflaged a particularly alien element that has crept into higher aristocracy. Look at the man who dictated the course of conduct of the Second World War, Lord Halifax, the British Ambassador to Washington. His son, Charles Wood, married a Miss Primrose, who is a blood relative of the most ignoble House of Rothschild. Behind such names as Lord Swaythling was hidden the name of Montague, associated with Queen Elizabeth, the majority stockholder of the Shell Oil Company. Nothing of course dare be said about the immense fortune she derives from the drug trade, a trade, which as I have shown, goes back to the 18th century.

One of the prime movers in the opium trade in China was Lord Palmerston, who clung obstinately to the belief that the trade would be allowed to continue.

In a letter from one of his men on the spot, a certain Mr. Elliott, said enough opium handed to the Chinese government would help to create a monopoly. Thereafter the British would withhold supplies, making the Chinese "coolie" pay more for his supplies. Then when the Chinese Government was on its knees, the British would once again offer to supply them at a higher price, thus retaining their monopoly through the Chinese government. But the plan did not succeed for very long. When the Chinese government responded by destroying large cargoes of opium stored in a warehouse, and the British merchants ordered to sign an agreement as individuals not to import any more opium into Canton city, they countered this by contracting various front companies to import on their behalf and it was not long before many of the ships in the roads of Macao, contained full cargoes of opium.

Chinese Commissioner Lin said:

> There is much opium on board the English vessels now lying in the roads of this place (Macao) which will never be returned to the country from whence it came. A sale must be made here on the coast, and I shall not be surprised to hear of its being smuggled in under American colors.

But to move on to more recent history of this infamous trade, which has been broadened to include vast amounts of cocaine, and legally produced drugs at enormous profits, such as Valium, and other so-called "prescription drugs." The oligarchist families of Great Britain moved their headquarters from Canton to Hong Kong, but remained in the same trade. They are still in it today in 2009 as a list of prominent names in the Colony will show.

As I said in my earlier works, a secondary industry arising from the opium trade made Hong Kong the most important gold trading center in the world. Gold is used to pay the peasants who produce the raw opium; after all what would a Chinese peasant do with as U.S. $100 bill? Opium produces 64 percent of the Gross National Product of China, which will give you some idea as to just how vast this "off ledger" business is. Unofficially it is estimated to be equal to the combined Gross National Product (GNP) of five of the smaller nations of Europe i.e. Belgium, Holland, the Czech Republic, Greece and Romania.

The Golden Triangle is perhaps the principal supplier of raw opium outside Afghanistan, although its position is being challenged by Pakistan, India, Lebanon and Iran. How do banks figure in this lucrative trade? It is a very long and complicated story, and the story will have to wait for another book. One way is the indirect method where banks finance the front companies importing the chemicals needed to process raw opium into heroin.

The Hong Kong and Shanghai Bank, with a large branch office in London is right in the middle of the business. A company called Tejapaibul banks with Hong Kong and Shanghai Bank, affectionately known as the "Hongshang Bank." What does this company do? It imports very large quantities of acetic anhydride, the essential chemical required in the refining process. This company is the major supplier of the acetic anhydride for the Golden Triangle. Financing of the trade is hived off to a subsidiary of the Hong Shang Bank, the Bangkok Metropolitan Bank. Thus the secondary activities connected to the opium trade in the Golden Triangle, while not as big as the actual trade in opium itself, nevertheless brings in a very substantial income to these banks.

I have been criticized for linking the price of gold with the ups and downs of the opium trade. Let us take a look at what happened in 1977, a critical year for gold. The Bank of China shocked the gold buffs and those clever forecasters who are to be found in vast numbers in America, by suddenly and without warning, releasing 80 tons of gold onto the market.

The experts didn't know that China had been buying and hoarding gold for a long time. That depressed the price of gold. All the experts could say was that they did not know the People's Republic of China possessed that much gold in the first place! Where did the gold come from? It came from the opium trade where it is a medium of "currency" in Hong Kong, but our gold price forecasting geniuses could not know that!

It was not only the British who are operating in the Golden Triangle. Substantial buyers (or their representatives) regularly travel to Hong Kong from all over the West to make buys. There is wholesale shipping of heroin out of Hong Kong harbor, heroin, which is destined to make its way into the West and be handed out at self-styled "rock" concerts. Red China is happy to co- operate with both sides in such a lucrative venture. Incidentally the policy of China toward England, vis-a-vis the drug trade, has changed little from what it was in the 19th century. The Chinese economy, tied to the economy of Hong Kong, would have taken a terrible beating, had an agreement not been reached.

One of the proofs of this is the loan accepted by China from the Standard and Chartered Bank. Since then the Matheson family has stepped forward and invested $300 million in a new real estate development being jointly developed by the Peoples Republic of China and the Matheson's banks. Wherever one looks in modern downtown Hong Kong - one sees towering new high-rise buildings, a testimony to the close links between the big banks, the opium trade and Red China.

I want to quote what the Venezuelan Ambassador to the U.N. said some time ago, and I think it is a very well thought-out statement:

> The problem of drugs has already ceased to be dealt with simply as one of public health or as a social problem. It has serious and far reaching which affects our national sovereignty; a problem of national security, because it strikes at the independence of the nation.

Drugs in all their manifestations of production, commercialization and consumption, de-nationalize and denaturalize everybody by injuring our ethical, religious and political life, our historic, economic and republican values. This is exactly the way in which the IMF and the Bank of International Settlement (BIS) are operating. I say without hesitation that these banks are nothing more than clearinghouses for the drug trade.

The BIS aids any country, which the IMF wants to sink, by setting up ways and means, which permits the easy flow of flight capital. Nor does the BIS recognize any distinctions when it comes down to what is "flight capital" and what is laundered drug money. Even if it could tell the difference, the BIS never says anything as its annual report for 2005 clearly indicated. Touching on the statement made by the Venezuelan Ambassador, we find that the BIS is seriously denationalizing many countries by interfering in their ethical, religious, economic and political life, through its demands via the IMF. And if any country, (including the U.S.) declines to bow the knee, BIS says in effect, "right, then we will blackmail you through narcotic dollars that we are holding for you in very large amounts." It is easy to see now why gold was demonetarized and substituted by paper "dollars" as the world's reserve currency. It is not so easy to blackmail a nation holding gold reserves as it is a nation holding worthless paper "dollars."

The International Monetary Conference mini summit held in Hong Kong and attended by an insider who is a source of mine, dealt with this very question, and from what was reported to me, the IMF is quite certain that it can do just that - blackmail nations with "dope dollars," who do not want to follow its conditions.

Rainer E. Gut of Credit Suisse said he foresaw a situation where national credit and national financing would soon be under a one umbrella organization. While he did not spell it out, it is clear what Gut was talking about, that is, under the BIS in a One World Government set-up. I do not want anyone to have any doubts whatsoever.

From Colombia to Miami, from Palermo to New York, from the Golden Triangle to Hong Kong, dope is big business. It is not a street corner penny-ante business. Now you know as well as I do, that successfully organizing the biggest business in the world, takes a great deal of money and expertise.

These talents are not found on the subways and street corners of New York though the pushers and peddlers are an integral and important part of the system, albeit only very small-time salesmen, who are easily replaceable. If a few are caught, or killed, what matter? There are plenty of replacements. No, it is not a small organization, but a vast empire, this dirty drug business. And of necessity it is operated from the top down, by the very top people in every country it touches.

If it were not so, like international terrorism, it would have been wiped out a long time ago — that it is not only still operating, but growing, should indicate to any reasonable man that this business has its foundations at the very highest levels.

The main countries involved in this, the biggest business in the world, are the USSR, Bulgaria, Turkey, Lebanon, the USA and France, Sicily, Southwest Asia, India, Pakistan, Afghanistan and Latin America, although not in order of importance. From the consumer point of sale, the USA, Europe and lately, the United Kingdom are the prime markets.

As I indicated, no dope is sold in the USSR, Iron Curtain countries or Malaysia. Many of the producer countries such as Turkey have very stiff penalties for drug users and small-time pushers. Some countries even carry the death penalty — strictly for the small fish, as a grandstand play to let the world see how "anti-drugs" they are.

The drug empire is divided between two "products," viz, the traditional heroin and the fairly recently arrived cocaine. There is a third category of drugs made by "legal" companies such as the notorious Hoffman La Roche, which companies make death dealing substances like LSD, Quaaludes and Amphetamines; the so called "uppers and downers" of what the street crowd call "the pill poppers paradise." Is this empire a loosely knit affair?

The answer appears to be a qualified "yes." There are exceptions. Kintex the notorious Bulgarian drug company is definitely a Bulgarian state-run company. Many of the banks handling the dirty money (and they know that it is dirty money) are well known multi-national banks, working through a network of subsidiaries.

The Kintex Company for instance has its own warehouses, fleets of trucks, including Common Market (EEC) international treaty-covered vehicles and a sophisticated network of couriers, including airline pilots and crews.

For those not familiar with the EEC, let me explain that TIR vehicles are Triangle International Routier trucks, clearly marked in this manner; they are supposed to carry only perishable goods. They are supposed to be inspected in the country of departure by that country's customs staff, and sealed with a special seal.

Under the international treaty obligations of member countries, these trucks are not to be stopped at borders, and are always passed through without inspection. It is a case of taking the Bulgarians and the Turks at their word, and hoping to God that the TIR trucks do not contain heroin, cocaine or raw opium, hash and or uppers and downers. The problem is that in many cases, TIR trucks do contain large caches of drugs.

After all, it is a well-known fact that the drug lords are no respecters of international treaties and in any case, can always get their paid stooges in other countries to substitute documents disguising the fact that the TIR truck originated in Sofia, Bulgaria.

The only way to stop these huge amounts of heroin and hash from getting through from the Far East is to end the TIR system. But that is exactly what it was set up to do! Forget about perishable goods and facilitating trade. That is just so much smoke in the eyes of the world. TIR equals dope in far too many cases. Remember that the next time you read about a big haul of heroin found in a false-bottom suitcase in Kennedy airport, and some unfortunate "mule" is arrested. That is strictly "small potatoes" for the news media.

There are other areas that grow poppies; Turkey, Pakistan and Iran. But as it has been for over three hundred years, the "best" stuff comes from India-Pakistan and Thailand. In these remote areas of high mountains and valleys, hill tribesmen grow the crop and gather the thick sap from the pod after it is cut with a razor blade.

Most of this is in the hands of wild Thai tribes, and in India, it is the Baluchi tribesmen who are the cultivators and the reapers of the "gold" cash crop. They call it "Golden Triangle," because the tribesmen insist on being paid in gold. To facilitate this, Credit Suisse began to sell 1 kilo of pure gold bars (what is called four ninths in the trade), as these small bars are easy to carry and trade readily. Most of this gold moves through Hong Kong, which trades more gold than New York and Zurich combined at the height of the "Dope Season," as it is known amongst Hong Kong gold traders. This area alone is thought to produce approximately 175 metric tons of pure heroin in a good year. The heroin is then pipelined to the Sicilian mafia and the French end of the business, for refining in the laboratories that infest the coast of France from Marseilles to Monte Carlo (and that includes the Grimaldi family — although I am not suggesting that there is a laboratory in their palace!)

The route followed goes through Iran and Turkey, as well as Lebanon. The Pakistan trade is via the Maccra coast. In Iran the "moving" is done by the Kurds, as it has always been done for centuries. One of the primary staging areas is of course Turkey, but lately Beirut has become immensely important, hence the war going on in that country, as each local baron tries to carve out his fiefdom the Swiss-Lebanese banks are right on hand to help with the money side of things. There are now very important refineries inside Turkey, which is a fairly recent development. Similarly in Pakistan, new laboratories, operating as "military-defense laboratories" are refining the raw opium, making it easier to transport on down the line.

Could this be the reason why the U.S. supports Pakistan and

not India; because certain banks have large investments in Pakistan, and it is not in curry powder or carpets! But the final and more elaborate refining is still carried out in laboratories in Turkey and along the French coast.

Now stop right there and consider what I have written. Is it possible, that with all the sophisticated techniques, methods and equipment available that law enforcement agencies cannot uncover and destroy these heroin factories? If this is the truth, then our intelligence services in the West are in need of Geriatric treatment, no, they must have died a long time ago, and we have forgotten to bury them!

Even a child could tell our drug enforcement agencies what to do. It would be a very simple matter to keep a check on all factories making acetic anhydride, the essential chemical component needed to refine heroin. It is so simple that it is laughable, and I am reminded of "Inspector Clouseau" of the "Pink Panther" cartoon and movie series. I think even that poor old Clesseau would be able to find the laboratories by following the route and destination of the acetic anhydride. Governments ought to make laws which would force manufacturers to keep a special register showing to whom the product is sold. But do not hold your breath on this one; remember the Dope Trade equals big business which is controlled by the oligarchy of Europe, England and the old "noble" families of America. Now don't get all fired up and tell me, "No, it isn't."

Of course the noble families of Britain and America are not going to advertise their goods in the shop window, and in such a dirty business one needs dirty people to run it, so ergo — the Mafia. The noble people never dirtied their hands during the China opium trade, and they have got a lot smarter since then. If perchance any of them should be apprehended, you would never get to hear about it and they would soon be released.

Is the dope trade run in a loosely knit organization? Again, a qualified yes, but remember, America and England are run by 300 families and they are all interfaced and intertwined through companies, banks and marriages, not to mention their ties to the Black Nobility. Although it is only a loosely knit entity, do not try to penetrate it.

If you go around asking questions in the wrong quarter, you run the risk of very strange things happening to you — that is if you are still intact. In equal, evenly spaced shipments, the "stuff comes down from Turkey and into Bulgaria. There it is repacked in TIR trucks and shipped to Trieste at the Adriatic Coast or the coast of France. Again, why not watch every single TIR truck in these two areas and place them under 24-hour surveillance? There are also sea routes and air routes, both well protected by "higher authority."

As I said, the odd mule is caught; sometimes even a large shipment is apprehended, not so much heroin (because it is more valuable); it is mainly cocaine and marijuana which is expendable as the cost of doing business. As weird as this may sound, "tips" often come from the very drug traders themselves where small amounts are involved.

In South America, the battle is against cocaine. The "manufacture" of cocaine is relatively simple and cheap, the base product easy to obtain at a low cost. Great fortunes can be made if one is willing to take the risk; not so much a risk involving law enforcement agencies as the risk of falling foul of the Cocaine Kings.

Interlopers are not welcome, and usually finish up as casualties in the "family feuds" that are constantly erupting. The principal cocaine producing countries are Colombia, Bolivia and Peru, with some attempts being made to introduce the coca bush to Brazil. In Colombia the drug mafia is a closely-knit family of gangsters who are well known to the authorities.

The problem is to do something about them. With protection from the highest sources in England and America, the cocaine barons are openly contemptuous of the efforts of sincere anti- drug fighters like President Betancourt of Colombia.

Betancourt did just about everything that his limited resources allowed, but it was not enough. The scourge of the cocaine dealers and producers continues to dominate Colombian national life. There seems to be no way to eradicate it. Betancourt fought a tremendous battle to survive. The drug barons, on the other hand, received every possible assistance from the IMF and it was no longer a question of whether Betancourt would survive; it was only a question of how long he could hang on to office. The other principal cocaine supplier to the United States is Bolivia and for a short while President Siles Zuazo tried to stem the tide of cocaine flowing into America, but his efforts failed. Here again, he was opposed every step of the way by the IMF and the Bank of International Settlement (BIS). Every one of his economic plans was declared "unacceptable" by the IMF. Labor unrest was fomented; strikes and "walk-outs" plagued his administration. Orchestrating this anti-Silas campaign were the crowned heads of the vipers of Europe. Silas did not enjoy the support of the Bolivian military; too many of the leading officers had been well paid by the cocaine barons before Silas came to power.

They missed the "perks" that went with the job. They did not care for the austerity imposed by the IMF. Matters came to a head on July 14, 1985, when Silas was ousted in national elections.

The former head of the country from 1971 to 1978, Hugo Banzer Suarez won handsomely. This was not unexpected as Suarez received very strong support from the Wall Street bankers and friends of Henry Kissinger, and of course, he got a vote of confidence from the Bolivian officer class.

As a former dictator and friend of the Bolivian Mafiosi, Suarez was expected to expand the cocaine trade. As a "reward" for the help he received from the IMF, Suarez was expected to enforce the brutal conditionality's imposed on Bolivia by the IMF, and as a result we saw many Bolivians die of starvation and hunger in the months that followed. This is of course all in accordance with the Global 2000 Report. At the same time, a veritable flood of cocaine began pouring into the U.S.

The IMF, acting on behalf of the hierarchy of the drug business in England and the USA, successfully forced Bolivia into chaos. In fact, the country was ungovernable during the period that elections were held. This is what the Venezuelan Ambassador meant when he said, "the drug trade is infringing on national sovereignty, on politics and economics." I can think of no clearer example of this than Bolivia. With the victory of Banzer, the IMF fairy godmother suddenly announced that it would back Bolivia in negotiations with foreign creditors. Bolivia's key industries are mining and agriculture. Both were in a state of bankruptcy, deliberately engineered by the IMF to oust Siles and punish him for his anti-cocaine trade stand. That the IMF was successful is all too apparent. Peru is another important producer of cocaine and also came under attack by the IMF because of its new leader's anti-cocaine stance. On August 2, 1985, the government announced a crackdown against illegal currency dealers, with over two hundred arrests, interest rates were cut and minimum wages increased by fifty percent.

This was absolutely contrary to IMF demands and conditions that called for stringent austerity measures. The IMF soon took action.

The guerilla movement, virtually crushed, suddenly began to take on a new energy and under its leader Abinal Guzman, went on a rampage that killed hundreds of peasants. Bomb blasts rocked Lima.

The economy was paralyzed. Sick of the chaos, the nation cried out for a strong leader. They found it in the person of Alberto Fujimora, Japanese-born citizen of Peru. Fujimora was a man of great honor and integrity, who looked to be the best hope of ridding Peru of the curse of the drug trade. Elected by a landslide, Fujimora faced the daunting task of battling the IMF and the BIS on the economic front, and the well financed and U.S. and British-supported Guzman and his guerilla army.

Chapter Two

Afghanistan's Role in the International Opium/Heroin Trade

Afghanistan is in the news once again simply because it is one of the principle sources of raw opium, as it has been ever since the days of the British East India Company (BEIC) the forbears of the Committee of 300. I will also examine the role played by Pakistan in the opium poppy culture, and why the United States has looked the other way on at least three occasions when the elected government of Pakistan was overthrown and replaced by a military regime, while Chile and Argentina were singled out for "special measures" for the same "crime."

Afghanistan is an ancient Muslim land north of the Hindu Kush Mountains. Some old instruments found in the Haibak Valley were carbon-dated, which showed they were at least a thousand years old. What attracted Westerners to the land is that it had the ideal climate and soil for the cultivation of opium-producing poppies. It was ruled by the Barakzai Dynasty from 1747 to 1929 and was known for prolonged conflict between members of the dynasty and tribal leaders.

Prior to the 18th century, the country was under the rule of Persia, and in parts, ruled by India. The Barakzai family has ruled the opium trade for at least 150 years, and as we know, when U.S. Armed Forces overthrew the Taliban, they placed a member of the clan, Hamid Barakzai, at the head of Afghanistan and the country is currently under his control.

In 1706, Kandahar declared its independence, and in 1709 Mir Vais, a Ghilzain chieftain, and a Sunnite Moslem defeated the Persian armies sent against him at Kandaha, which ensured that the opium trade was kept in British hands.

In 1715 Mir Abdullah succeeded Mir Vais, but was caught trying to make peace with the Persians, and overthrown in 1717. There followed a period of intense rivalry followed by an invasion of Persia by the Afghans.

In 1763 Zaman Shah, son of Timur came to power, but instead of unity, it was marked by total and incessant tribal rivalries and fierce battles. His father, a timid ruler, could not stop India from taking some of its territories, including the Punjab, which was lost to the Sikhs during the battles of 1793-1799.

In 1799, emissaries from the BEIC began arriving in Kandahar to meet with the ruler, Shah Shuja. In 1809, before the death of Shah Shuja, the BEIC concluded an agreement with him that it would help to repel "foreigners" particularly from Persia and India. In 1818 Mahmud Shah assumed control of the country and set about strengthening relations with the BEIC, who by then were in charge of "agricultural expansion" in the form of vast poppy fields. Sensing that a rich prize awaited them, the Persians invaded in 1816, but were driven out by Path All Kahn a soldier and confidant of the BEIC.

In 1818 there was a revolt among the tribes over the cultivation of poppies and the revenues derived from the sale of raw opium to the BEIC. As a result, Afghanistan was divided up into tribal enclaves, Kabul, Kandahar and Ghazni etc. It was during this time of division that India stole Kashmir from Afghanistan, because India wanted a piece of the lucrative opium pie. In 1819 after a series of tribal wars Dost Mohammed captured Kabul and became the ruler of Ghazni and Kandahar. Seeing a chance to horn in on the opium trade, which flourished under the BEIC, Persia attacked Herat in 1837 and a tribal conflict broke out that lasted until July 1838. The root cause of the fighting was the opium trade, firmly in the hands of the British. Ever the master- schemers, the British Government concluded an agreement with Ranjit Singh and Shah Suju, who under the auspices of the BEIC would restore the throne of Shah Shuja, thus unifying the tribesmen, and effectively blocking out Persia. But unbeknown to the British, Dost Mohamed was becoming rich by dipping into the opium trade, making deals outside of BEIC.

In 1839, British troops stationed in India moved into Afghanistan in the First Afghan War. They deposed Dost Mohammed and banished him to India. His assets were seized by BEIC and British troops took over the major cities and towns, but soon found that they were dealing with an elusive force of tribesmen under one or another alliance.

Throughout this entire period, nothing was allowed to get in the way of poppy cultivations, and large amounts of raw opium were dispatched out of Afghanistan, usually through what was to become Pakistan. During this period, because the company knew how to control local tribesmen and secure protection for their lucrative investments, the company made huge profits. Questions were raised in the

House of Commons in London, as to why British troops were being deployed in such a forlorn country as Afghanistan when there was nothing of significance to keep them there. Little did the poor Members of Parliament (MPs) know about the vast fortune being made every year by BEIC. While the British advertised their fight with the Chinese "war lords" (in reality the Customs officers of the government of China) they kept their wars in Afghanistan a closely guarded secret.

When war broke out against the British by tribesmen under Dost Mohammed, it was passed off as a "tribal skirmish" in the British newspapers, if it was mentioned at all. A British force on a march to Kandahar was attacked by Dost Mohammed's forces, which were beaten back, their leader taken prisoner and exiled to India.

In 1842, Sir Alexander Burns placed Shah Shuja on the throne again. London thought the action would placate the tribesmen, but, instead it led to a great deal of unrest culminating in the murder of Sir Alexander and a British envoy by the name of Sir William McNaughton. This was the signal for a general revolt against British rule, and Lord Auckland sent a British force of 16,000 British and Sepoy troops to occupy Kabul. But the revolt was so severe that the British forces had to retreat from Kabul to Kandahar. But on the road back, the British forces walked into an ambush by 3000 tribesmen who inflicted many casualties on them. Also killed was Shah Shuja, whom the tribesmen believed was a puppet for the British.

The Afghanis now took control of the opium poppy fields and various warlords began asserting their control of the opium routes out of the country. Worse than that, they began exacting tribute from BEIC caravans crossing into

India.

Caravans of pack animals loaded with raw opium were attacked when tribute was not paid, and the opium stolen, with many killed by the warlords. It was during these episodes that Rudyard Kipling wrote his tales of daring about the British forces guarding the route through the Khyber Pass. The ordinary British citizen thrilled to these tales of bravery. They had no idea that British soldiers were being sacrificed on behalf of a private multi-billion dollar enterprise, which had nothing to do with "God, the Queen and Country."

During this period the warlords were loosely affiliated under the leadership of Akbar Kahn, son of Dost Mohammed.

In 1842 a British Army force under the command of Sir George Pollock came up from India and retook Kabul. Hundreds of tribesmen thought to have part in the attack that cost the British Army so dearly, were summarily executed. Dorst Mohammed was again placed on the throne by Sir George. He at once set about defeating the opium tribal factions and punished those who had taken over BEIC poppy fields.

Because of his "noble" work, on March 30, 1855, the British government signed the Treaty of Peshawar with Mohammed, thus enabling him to control Kandahar and Kabul, but not the important Helmet opium poppy cultivations fields at Herat, which the Persians had seized from the BEIC. Even so, the BEIC trade of raw opium produced in Afghanistan began to rival that of the Ganges Valley and Benares.

Britain thereupon declared war on Persia. The innocent British public was told that the war was over Persia trying to take over British colonial territory. By 1857 the Persians were beaten and opted for peace through a treaty signed in Paris wherein they recognized the "independence" of Afghanistan and gave up claims to heart. British puppet Dost Mohammed was sent to take control of Herat, but tribal rivalry kept the area in turmoil for the next five years, with Dost only able to bring it under British jurisdiction in 1863. If the British learned anything at all about Afghanistan it was this: Never presume to have an area under control until every faction was in agreement with each other, and that could take a lifetime. Herat was a good example. It took a ten-month siege to pry loose the hold of one of the tribesmen of the region. Just when they thought they had everything "pacified," Dost died in 1870, and almost immediately, Herat was plunged into civil war when the brother of Dost, one Sher Ali, tried to assert his claims to succession. When he could not get the tribes to agree on anything, Ali called on Russia for help, having lost faith in the British, and in June of 1878, a Russian mission under General Stolietov arrived in Kabul. The alarm was immediately sounded by BEIC and once again the parties went to war as Sher All refused to accept a British mission counter-offer. The war lasted for a year (1878- 1879) during which Sher Ali was killed. Deeply alarmed that the Russians might bring their lucrative opium trade with Afghanistan to a halt, British forces invaded the entire area under their puppet Yakub, son of Sher Ali. British forces then spread out and garrisoned the whole country. At that point a treaty was signed whereby the British would pay a "protection fee" of $75,000 annually, to guarantee unmolested passage of the opium caravans through the Khyber Pass, where British troops were stationed to help enforce the agreement.

Of course Rudyard Kipling's tales said nothing about why convoys were being guarded by Her Majesty's troops, and no doubt there would have been hell to play had the true mission of the troops been revealed.

Basking in what they thought was a complete success of their mission to Kabul, the British forces began to relax their vigilance as there were no more raids on poppy fields and no attacks on convoys through the Khyber Pass. But there was a rude awakening for London lurking in the background. On September 3, 1879, Sir Louis Cavagnari (a scion of the old Black Nobility of Venice) was murdered along with his escort, and the country was once again plunged into another war. Yakub, who was accused of conspiring with rebel tribesmen behind the backs of the British and was removed on October 19, 1879.

In 1880 when the British were preparing for war against the Boer Republics in South Africa to rob that country of its massive gold resources, a new Afghan leader came on the scene, one Abd-Ar-Rahman, a nephew of Ali Sher Ali. The British were happy with the new man, who had great success in keeping the peace and imposing his authority on the ever bickering tribal factions.

In this period of relative stability, a vast amount of high-quality raw opium flowed out of the country into the storehouses of the BEIC. It is believed that during this period, (1880-1891), billions of pounds flowed into the BEIC coffers, enough to pay ten times more than the cost of the Anglo-Boer War, which broke out in 1899. There was also a great deal of interference by Russia in an attempt to gain a foothold in Afghanistan and provide a buffer for its borders. Russia did not have any interest in the opium trade; its sole concern was to gain a territorial buffer. Finally, after five years of severe problems with Britain, the two countries reached an accord in which Russia agreed to stay out of Afghan's affairs.

Throughout its turbulent history, Afghanistan continued to produce some of the highest grades of raw opium, much sought after by Western users and the principle route through which this cargo was moved was through Pakistan. Afghanistan's history of opium is therefore tied tightly to the history of the opium trade in Pakistan and its transit routes to the coast and onwards to the Middle East and Western Europe.

At the height of its power, BEIC received 4000 tons of opium every year from Afghanistan. The estimated value of this huge production in one year (1801) was $500 million, a staggering fortune in those days. Most of the opium was moved through the Khyber Pass into India (which part is today called Pakistan) and thence down to the desolate Maccra coastline, where it is picked up by Arab dhows and taken to Dubai, there to be paid for in gold. No paper money for this trade is ever acceptable. As the result of this trade, there are no less than 25 banks in Dubai who trade in gold, among which the British Bank of the Middle East is the largest in the gold for opium trade. The Moslems of Afghanistan, unlike the Chinese worker class, do not use opium and thus did not become addicted to it. They were happy to produce crops of poppies, extract the opium sap, form in into crude opium and then sell it. Thus Afghanistan escaped the ravages of the terrible plague of addition to opium that eventually overcame China. Then, as now, the business of growing the poppies and collecting the much-prized sap are the dominant occupation of the male population of Afghanistan.

Secrets are carefully preserved, and as long as all things are equal, it will be thus until the end of time! I saw fields of poppies nursed from seedlings to full grown flowering plants - and then when the sap in the pods rose, how they were sliced with razors from which the rubber like resin flowed and congealed. I also saw that there was no attempt to curb or reduce poppy cultivation. I have gone to some lengths to provide details of what kind of rule was forced on Afghanistan by foreign powers, in the hope readers will understand that very little has changed in the intervening years. The United States believes that by its invasion and bombing, the country has been subdued, but in this the United States is sadly mistaken. Afghanistan is a country of warlords and competing factions all trying to get a share of the opium, a picture of confused loyalties and intense rivalries. This, the United States and its allies will never be able to defeat.

The Taliban — created, armed and directed by the Central Intelligence Agency (CIA) as a counterforce to prevent Russia taking over the country — are now the enemy! When the Taliban came to power, they were derided, mocked and scorned, but they soon asserted themselves and after defeating the Russians, turned on their American benefactors, ordering the cessation of poppy-growing and export of raw opium. Mile after mile of poppy fields were burned along with stocks of the opium. Suddenly, the lords of the drug trade in the City of London and on Wall Street saw a huge loss of income looming, and the situation had to be drastically turned around.

I cannot say for certain how the attack on the World Trade center came about, but one thing I do know is that the American people would never have accepted an invasion of Afghanistan by U.S. forces had it not been for the disaster of September 11, 2001, so it is more than likely that history will reveal the 9/11 tragedy as a "contrived situation." Much to the consternation of the banks in Dubai, and the opium traders in the United States and Britain, the Taliban cleared out the warlords led by the Barakzai clan who had been pumping opium to the West and most of whom fled to Pakistan or into the mountainous sections of the country. The opium trade came to a screeching halt. The Taliban passed a decree that anyone growing poppies or trading in opium would be shot. The warlord opium bosses scattered along with their criminal stooges.

That sent the alarm bells ringing all over Westminster and New York. In Dubai, the 90 banks servicing the opium trade saw ruin staring them in the face. Something had to be done, and it was. The United States went to war against Afghanistan, just as the British, Russians and the Persians before them. The purpose of the war, we are told, was to "root out the Taliban and their al- Qaeda terrorists." A huge squadron of bombers flew sorties around the clock and the few remaining buildings left standing in Kandahar after the war with Russia, were reduced to impressive piles of rubble. War hawks Rumsfeld, Wolfowitz, Cheney and Perle were jubilant. At home, the New York papers trumpeted the news that the U.S. had "won" the war in Afghanistan. Little did the American people know that the war had only just started. American troops will have to stay in Afghanistan for decades, to keep the opium factions apart and to ensure the smooth flow of opium through the ancient trade routes. The top military brass of Pakistan's army will benefit greatly from the cocaine flowing out of Afghanistan, even as they have always done. That is why Pervez Musharraf was selected as our top "ally in the war against terrorism."

With the Taliban gone and the Barakzai clan once again in

control, the opium trade is flourishing in Afghanistan after the fall of the Taliban and it is unclear whether the new government will try to stop or at least curtail it. We venture to suggest that under the rule imposed by the U.S., opium trade will not only regain its past production, but also actually increase the amount of raw opium produced. In its annual report on the international drug trade, the State Department said the Taliban, driven out of power by the U.S. military in 2005, virtually eliminated opium poppy cultivation in the regions under their control.

Overall opium production fell dramatically, to about 74 tons in 2001 from about 3,656 tons in 2000 and almost all the production was in parts of Afghanistan held by the Northern Alliance, Washington's ally in the war against the Taliban. There you have it straight from the horse's mouth: Our "war on drugs" is as false as a counterfeit Federal Reserve note. While the Taliban were destroying crops and stocks of opium, the CIA was assuring our "allies" - the so-called "War Lords," an assortment of low-life and cutthroat murdering gangsters - not to worry, they would soon be back in power. The Drug Enforcement Agency (DEA) did not try to go in and crush this gang of vermin while they had a remarkable opportunity to do so. Instead, the U.S. protected the drug-dealing thugs. Afghanistan has traditionally been one of the world's major producers of opiates, along with India, which regained its place in 2008 as top producer because of the Taliban ban. Opium is the raw material for the opiates heroin and morphine, and Afghanistan has been the major supplier of those drugs to the region and to Western Europe and the United States. A recently released U.S. report said widespread cultivation of poppies resumed in Afghanistan after the collapse of the Taliban and drug traffickers remained active in Afghanistan, this in spite of the massive on the ground presence of U.S. Armed Forces. Although the interim authority in Kabul, the Cheney, Rumsfeld and Wolfowitz puppet, Hamid Karzai (Barakzai) backed by the United States, announced its own ban on growing opium, the ban hardly ran beyond the capital and was not worth the paper it is was written on. Had Karzai tried to enforce his decree he would have been found one morning with his throat cut from ear to ear. His gangster dealers would never allow him to remain alive to interfere with their lucrative business.

The report said:

> The Authority lacks means to enforce its ban, and it must work with local power centers and the donor community if the ban is actually to be respected. It remains uncertain whether the urgings and even the financial support of the international community will be sufficient to eliminate poppy cultivation in Afghanistan quickly... In the wake of hostilities, which faction is actually in control in which region, varies. Whether factions will follow a ban on poppy cultivation issued by the Interim Authority is uncertain.

What utter nonsense.

What about enforcing it through the presence of a large number of DEA agents backed by the U.S. military? We know that our controllers fully believe that the American people are the most gullible in the world, but to try and foist such nonsense on the people and think it would be believed, goes beyond explanation. The Northern Alliance, which dominates Karzai's government, does not appear to have taken any action against drugs in the parts of the country that it does control. There have also been several UN reports of farmers cultivating a second opium crop in Northern

Alliance-controlled areas, the report continued.

Can you believe the audacity of these people in expecting us to believe such patent absurdity? "Does not appear?" The fact is that even while the Taliban were doing their utmost to eradicate the scourge, not only did Washington know that their "allies" were growing poppies, but actually assured them that no one would interfere with their trade, as long as they were our "ally" in the war against the Taliban. Washington thereupon set about arming and training them to go to war against the whole of Afghanistan while leaving their deadly, death-dealing trade intact. These are the real facts behind the war in Afghanistan.

The United States is putting some hope in regional efforts to stop Afghan opiates leaving the country through the Six Plus Two group, that brings together the United States, Russia and Afghanistan's six immediate neighbors. This is another charade. Nothing is being done and nothing will ever be done to stop the Afghan opium trade. If there were to be a serious effort in this direction, the leader of Pakistan, General Pervez Musharraf, would be thrown out of a job. Half of the Pakistan ruling establishment is totally dependent on tolls on the lucrative opium revenues derived from the opium traffic passing through Pakistan on its way to Europe and the United States. In the meantime, narcotics trafficking in Helmand will continue, despite the best efforts of the Interim Authority and the international community, the State Department report added. There is absolutely no proof that Afghanistan's Taliban rulers were ever involved in the opium trade, there is no evidence that drugs are a major source of funding for Osama bin Laden's al- Qaeda network. We have searched every known record and found no such evidence. We dismiss the State Department's allegations as propaganda, plain and simple.

But the officials said the al-Qaeda network, based in Afghanistan, benefits indirectly from the Taliban's involvement in trafficking and they are concerned that it could develop closer links with traffickers as it comes under pressure from the United States following the September 11 terrorist attacks. Where is the proof? Allegations do not constitute proof, and thus far no proof has been presented. What we have here is propaganda intended to throw doubt on the religious beliefs of the Taliban.

> "Whenever you have a terrorist organization that has to have sources of money and they are geographically alongside drug organizations that produce money, then there's obviously the potential for a stronger connection between the two,"

Asa Hutchinson, a former head of the DEA told the House Government Reform subcommittee on criminal justice, drug policy and human resources. Well now, our response is that Mr. Hutchinson's appointment was a political one, and he knows little if anything about the drug trade, having spent his time in the House of Representatives before losing his seat, because of his role in the Clinton impeachment proceedings.

U.S. officials said that opium trafficking has been a major source of financing for the Taliban, the hard line Islamic militia that governs most of the country. Hutchinson and William Bach, State Department counter-narcotics official, said Taliban guards sometimes accepted raw opium instead of cash.

This pathetic claim comes straight out of the mouths of the ruffians comprising the "Northern Alliance," who cannot tell the truth because if they did, they would lose their favorable status with Washington. Here is another "gem:"

> In anticipation of U.S. military reprisals for the terrorist attacks, the Taliban appears to be dumping its stockpiles. Opium prices in the region dropped suddenly from $746 a kilogram to $95 immediately after the attacks. It has since bounced back to $429.

One would think that having told us that the Taliban needed arms, they would hardly have "dumped" their most direct means of purchasing them! In any case, there is no proof that the Taliban has ever traded in opium. Those who might have been tempted would have been subject to summary trial and execution under their religious code. By the late 1790s, Afghanistan became the world's leading producer of opium, the raw material for heroin. At its peak, it supplied more than 70 percent of the revenues of the BEIC, a distinction the country held through both world wars, right up to the late 1990s.

When they came to power, the Taliban ordered a halt to opium cultivation, citing religious principles. International observers confirmed production had been almost wiped out in Taliban- held areas, with the little remaining opium being cultivated on land held by the so-called opposition "Northern Alliance," a gang of scoundrels, drug dealers and murderers under the protection of former Secretary of Defense, Donald Rumsfeld.

Does this not explain a great many things that need explaining? And it is not the first time the U.S. has been directly involved in winking at the dope trade. We saw it in Vietnam, Lebanon, Mexico, Pakistan and now, Afghanistan. But U.S. officials say the ban had little effect on trafficking because the Taliban hasn't eliminated massive opium stockpiles from previous years or stopped traffickers. What is the truth? We have the State Department and the new boss of the DEA telling us that the Taliban "dumped" their massive stocks of opium, and in the same breath we are supposed to believe the Taliban did no such thing! Believe us when we say that there would have been no need to "dump" stocks. The Pakistan dope lords -- including those in the military — would have purchased every kilo of raw opium from the Taliban at full price.

The whole story is unadulterated rubbish. What happened was that the prime movers in the trade were all in an area "protected" by the Northern Alliance and the Taliban could not get in there because Donald Rumsfeld had armed them with tanks, artillery and all the accoutrements of a modern army, courtesy of the taxpayers. Subcommittee chairman Mark Souder, R- Indiana, called the Taliban ban

> "a coldly calculated ploy to control the world market price for their opium and heroin."

It looks as if it is a case of the blind leading the blind! Souder sounds worse than Hutchinson. Why not just tell the truth and let the American people decide? Why tell lies and confuse the picture? "U.S. officials have estimated that opium could provide the Taliban with up to $50 million a year," Hutchinson and Bach said. Al-Qaeda benefits indirectly because it has been protected by the Taliban.

But Bach said that drug trafficking "just doesn't seem to be the major resource for al-Qaeda," while Souder noted that U.S. officials have paid little attention to the Afghan opium trade because little of it entered the United States:

> We now must confront the new reality that the Afghan

drug trade, largely without crossing our borders, has harmed our country just as much as the drugs from half a world away that reached American streets.

If the average American can make sense of these conflicting statements, then we will be very surprised. But whether we can make sense of it or not, it is, and we repeat, unadulterated double talk. We ask you once again to consider the following:

➢ We are told that the Taliban "dumped" the bulk of its opium stocks.

➢ We are told that the Taliban needed opium-derived revenues.

➢ We are told that the Taliban were provided with $50 million a year from opium revenues.

➢ We are told that the Taliban "dumped" its massive stocks. Did this amount to $50 million dollars being "dumped?" Why would anyone want to "dump" $50 million?

➢ We are told that hitherto the DEA has paid little attention to the principal supplier of raw opium in the world. Does this make sense? If the DEA did not pay attention to the opium streaming out of Afghanistan, then the DEA is guilty of dereliction of duty.

➢ We are told that the reason the DEA is in dereliction of duty is because so little of that opium reaches the United States!

Can you believe these people? They must think the American people are the most stupid people in the world. After the September 11 attacks in New York and

Washington, Afghanistan was at the center of the world's attention. The "alliance against terrorism" led by the United States bombed Afghanistan and elements of the al-Qaeda fled the country and Afghan illicit opium cultivation became an element in the propaganda war. The heroin trade was brought up repeatedly as one of the main sources the networks of Osama bin Laden. But somehow, we were led to believe, bin Laden escaped and remains at large in Afghanistan, still directing terrorism against the West. This has to be treated with a good deal of skepticism, in our opinion.

> "The arms the Taliban are buying today are paid for with the lives of young British people buying their drugs on British streets. That is another part of their regime that we should seek to destroy,"

former British Prime Minister Tony Blair said. His statement is an example of the distorting declarations made on real situations with regard to the opium economy inside Afghanistan. Actually, it is Mr. Blair's ally in Afghanistan, the "Northern Alliance" who is profiting more from the criminal opium economy every day. No proof has been shown that the Taliban deals in opium at all.

When former Prime Minister Blair had the British Army in Afghanistan, there was plenty of time to eradicate poppy fields, conduct search and destroy missions against stocks of raw opium. Why did Mr. Blair not order his troops to take that action? It was a great opportunity to make a coordinated sweep across the land and put poppy cultivators out of business, arrest the dealers and destroy their stocks. The means and the money was there to undertake such an operation, but no, apparently Mr. Blair felt his words were more powerful than his deeds. This is known as "propaganda." Blair must know what Souder and Hutchinson said. They apparently are not bothered by the death of young British heroin addicts, because it does not affect America! Believe this stuff at risk of losing your IQ level. When the Taliban took power in Kabul in 1996, they merely inherited a situation that had transformed Afghanistan since the late 18th/19th centuries into the world's largest opium producer. Between 1994 and 1998, opium output totaled between an annual 2,000 and 3,000 metric tons of raw material. The majority of this was shipped through India (later Pakistan) at first guarded by the finest the British Army could muster and immortalized in the tales of derring-do spun by Rudyard Kipling. Later it was the Pakistani Army generals who stood guard over the lucrative income the trade provided them. Once the opium-for-gold swap took place in Dubai, the raw opium was refined into heroin and morphine in Turkey and France. Only a very tiny fraction of the opium was processed inside Afghanistan. All previous records were broken in 1999 and 2000 when opium production in Afghanistan reached 4500 tons.

The Bush administration would have us believe that on July 27, 2000 "... after many years of international pressure, Taliban leader Mullah Omar issued a total ban on opium planting for the next season." This is not so. The Taliban banned opium poppy cultivation and production of raw opium immediately upon taking power. World pressure had nothing to do with it.

If "world pressure" was the reason why the Taliban banned the trade, why did "world pressure" not have any effect prior to the advent of the Taliban? Cultivation went down in Taliban controlled territories, while it flourished in areas under control of the "Northern Alliance." The rapid advance of U.S. forces due to the massive bombing campaign of the United States in its war against the Bin Laden network and the takeover of Kabul by the "Northern Alliance" gangsters, by no means ended the opium economy. On the contrary, the exact opposite happened; there was a resurgence of the opium economy although the U.S. and its British ally were now in control of all major poppy cultivation areas. Afghanistan became the center of attention of the United Nations International Drug Control Program (UNDCP) ever since it became clear that the country had gained the status of the world's largest source of opium, and this was twenty years before the Taliban arrived on the scene. UNDCP projects aimed at stemming the Afghanistan flow of illicit opium had no measurable impact. In the so-called "war on opium" in Afghanistan, the major cultivation areas were under the control of the so-called "Northern Alliance," a name dredged up by Rumsfeld to cover its true composition of bandits and thugs.

Since 1994, the Annual Opium Poppy Survey of UNDCP's Crop Monitoring Program is the most reliable source for figures on poppy cultivation and opium production potential. The most recent one, released in October 2008, confirmed the dramatic fall in opium poppy cultivation in detail that is to say, after the Taliban took control. Before that, "world pressure" had made no impact on the opium lords who were later to be drafted into Rumsfeld's so-called "Northern Alliance."

To understand the complexities of the Afghan opium economy, UNDCP's Strategic Study Series is fairly useful although giving no details of behind the scenes controllers. It documents the expansion of poppy fields in Afghanistan and the reasons behind it; the role of opium as a source of credit and in livelihood strategies of small farmers and war refugees; the role of women in the opium economy and the rural dynamics behind the illicit trade, which earned billions of pounds for the BEIC and which still earns a substantial fortune for those in the distribution of opium, such as the Pakistani army generals. The latest issue of U.N. Drug Council Program (UNDCP) Global Illicit Drug Trends (2008) under the supervision of Sandeep Chawla, head of UNDCP's Research Section, features a special section on Afghanistan, with a fairly useful but limited overview of opium economy trends since the early days explaining how Afghanistan became the largest opium supplier in the world.

In my book, *The Committee of 300*, I gave a detailed account of how this giant group was able to make so much money out of the misery of the opium trade forced upon the Chinese people by the government of Great Britain. The book provides a detailed account of the history of the vile trade of opium and heroin trafficking in the area, including deals sanctioned by the CIA and Pakistani ISI intelligence agency during the jihad against the Soviet occupation in the 1980s. There are many "establishment" reports on the criminalized Afghan economy, largely devoted to explaining two decades of smuggling trends before and after 1989, which attempt to give the impression that the opium- smuggling trade is a relatively new thing.

Most of them mention 1987-1989 as the "starting date" of the opium trade and ancillary spin-off illegal pursuits, whereas the documents found in the British Museum and in India House show that the illicit trafficking in heroin and morphine began with the arrival of the British in Afghanistan. India (later Pakistan) was deeply implicated in the criminal trade starting under British rule in 1868 and continuing to this day. The following is quoted as an example to the tepid nature of establishment reporting:

> Not only has Afghanistan become the world's largest opium producer and a center for arm dealing, but it supports a multi-billion dollar trade in goods smuggled from Dubai to Pakistan. This criminalized economy funds both the Taliban and their adversaries. It has transformed relations and weakened states and legal economies throughout the region. Sustainable peace — will require not just an end to fighting and a political agreement but a regional economic transformation that provides alternative forms of livelihood and promotes accountability.

On the face of it, everything in the report is tepid and identifies no one. But its goals seem to be possible, although in reality, opium has ruled Afghanistan and Pakistan (that part which was formerly India) since 1625 and nothing is going to change that. And here is the end of the tale: Nothing will be done by the U.S. and its so-called "Northern Alliance partners" to put an end to the lucrative trade on which no less that 23 British banks in Dubai depend for profits and for their very existence, and from which banks, the profit is funneled to banks in the City of London. How naive to believe that these super-banks will allow anyone to interfere with their money making machine.

British East India Company documents at India House London, (before it was mysteriously destroyed) provided unique insights into Afghanistan's opium trade and detailed the Northern trafficking routes from Afghanistan, through Pakistan and on to Dubai. It was never considered a "criminal trade" during the days of the BEIC. The only "criminal activity" recorded in these documents was about bandits trying to hijack opium mule trains passing through the Khyber Pass, where they were repelled by the finest of the British Army. U.S. figures about Afghanistan have been inaccurate and strongly political over the past twenty years. Interestingly, in these recent statements, for the first time the DEA uses almost exclusively UNDCP figures, which they considered grossly overestimated, at least until a few years ago.

We wonder why? Now, it is politically expedient to cite statistics as part of the U.S. ploy to discredit the Taliban and to merge the "War on Terror" with the "War on Drugs." However in reality, neither exists; but the charade has to be kept going to provide an excuse for draconian, thoroughly unconstitutional "laws," which flagrantly violate the Bill of Rights. That is why we can't find Bin Laden. If we did, suddenly, there would be no Taliban and no reason for the "war on terrorism" to continue. In Afghanistan, with the Taliban gone, harvest time is a non-event for growers of opium in Afghanistan and Pakistan, a region now rivaling South East Asia as the world's biggest source of heroin, the drug derived from the opium poppy plants.

The G.W. Bush administration opted not to destroy the opium crop in Afghanistan. Rather oddly, President Bush, who previously linked the Afghan drug trade directly to terrorism, abruptly decided not to destroy the Afghan opium crop. A U.S. intelligence official who returned from Afghanistan reported this to a European news magazine. The source, who requested that he not be identified, noted that the opium poppy fields are blooming and ready for harvest. U.S. forces could destroy the crops using aerial spraying techniques, but no such action is planned. There are no flamethrowers being directed against the ripening poppy buds, no signs of troops pulling up the plants and burning them. In fact, in the poppy fields, all is peaceful, as the farmers know that nobody is going to bother them. Nor do they care about "terrorism" in far away lands, but some intelligence agents are deeply worried by the U.S. ban on destroying opium poppy fields.

The January 2002 U.N. report on drug trafficking stated:

> If the estimated 3,000 tons of opium reaches market, it will lead to a new upsurge in international terrorism and a great loss in international credibility for the Bush administration and the United States' ability to conduct war in the 21st century. America's enemies throughout the world from China to North Korea to Iran will be emboldened by this lack of strategic vision and political will. The U.S. and all its allies signed onto a worldwide ban on opium sales. In January 2002, the U.N. issued a report on the Afghan opium production, noting that allied forces needed to act quickly to destroy the 2002 opium poppy crops before the end of spring. The U.S. and British forces took no such action.

The global importance of the ban on opium poppy cultivation and trafficking in Afghanistan is enormous. Afghanistan has been the main source of illicit opium: 70 percent of global illicit opium production in 2000 and up to 90 percent of heroin in European drug markets originated from Afghanistan. There are reliable indications that opium poppy cultivation has resumed since October 2001 in some areas (such as the southern provinces Uruzgan, Helmand, Nangarhar and Kandahar), following the effective implementation of the Taliban ban on cultivation in 2001, not only because of the breakdown in law and order, but also because the farmers are desperate to find a means of survival following the prolonged drought.

Intelligence sources say that the CIA opposes the destruction of the Afghan opium poppy crop, because to do so would result in the overthrow of the Pakistani government. According to these sources, Pakistani intelligence had threatened to overthrow President Musharraf in the event that he ordered crops to be destroyed. The history of Pakistan makes us believe this to be no idle threat. Former Pakistan President A.H. Bhutto was judicially hanged for trying to end the trade and his successor, General Zia ul Haq, died in a very mysterious plane crash after skimming money from the top, money that was earmarked for City of London banks. The threat to overthrow Musharraf is motivated in part by Islamic radical groups linked to the Pakistani intelligence service, Inter-Services Intelligence (ISI). The radical groups reportedly obtain their primary funding through opium production and trade. The top brass of the Pakistani Army is deeply involved in guarding the passage of opium through their country - as it has been all along — and would brook no interruption of the trade. Pakistan's intelligence service is utterly corrupt and unreliable, not to mention unstable and disloyal. They will go to the highest bidder and to hell with religious principles. The CIA has been in bed with them for many years and is unlikely to change course. As Bhutto bitterly concluded:

> If they [the CIA] are in fact opposing the destruction of the Afghan opium trade, it'll only serve to perpetuate the belief that the CIA is an agency devoid of morals; off on their own program rather than that of our constitutionally elected government. If we don't take this opportunity to destroy the opium production in Afghanistan, we are worse than the Taliban, who did stop it despite claims to the contrary.

The CIA's decision not to stop the Afghan opium production has been approved by the Committee of 300, their ultimate boss. According to intelligence sources, both the U.K. and French governments have quietly given their approval of the American policy. The CIA has a history of supporting international drug trafficking and acted almost identically during the Vietnam War, which had catastrophic consequences — a big increase in the heroin trade in the U.S. beginning in the 1970s was directly attributable to the CIA. The famous interview given by Chou En Lai to the Egyptian newspaper Al Ahram supports the contention that CIA has been complicit in the global drug trade for years. That is the way the Committee of 300 wants things to go, and according to intelligence sources, a simple grant of $2000 a year, no more than $20 million in total, paid directly to Afghan farmers would stop all opium production. The U.S. war in Afghanistan has already cost an estimated $40 billion, with not one penny spent on eradicating poppy fields and interdicting the flow of raw opium into Pakistan. (2009 figures U.S. State Department.)

Now that we know the millions of dollars wasted on U.S. advertising campaigns linking illegal drug sales to terrorism were deceitful, and now that we know that the Bush administration protected Afghanistan's opium production, we begin to get a good idea about just how wrong the war in Afghanistan is, and why the U.S. chose Pakistan to be "our major ally in the fight against terrorism." Ending opium production in Afghanistan would not cost one-tenth of the millions of dollars spent on TV advertising about our "war on terror - war on drugs," but the strange lack of action in Afghanistan against the drug trade by Rumsfeld the "war hawk" and the Bush administration in general, shows how hypocritical and flawed the so-called "war on terror" is. Every time you see some talking head like Bill O'Reilly announcing another successes in seizing terrorist money, just remember that it is but a drop in the ocean compared with the billions of dollars flowing into the coffers of the Committee of 300 banks in Dubai, and know that it will not make a scrap of difference to the flow of illegal Afghan opium money into City of London banks and offshore banks, not to mention the flow of heroin into America. The war in Afghanistan is not won. Our troops will never come home. The opium trade has to be guarded.

The United Nations Office of Drugs and Crime (UNODC) published its Rapid Assessment Survey of opium poppy cultivation in Afghanistan. The Federal government in Washington DC also published its annual Drivers of Opium Cultivation report. Responding, British Foreign Office Minister Kim Howells said:

> The U.K. government wants to reduce the heroin reaching our streets from Afghanistan. The scale of the drugs trade in Afghanistan is enormous and the strategy to wipe out the trade will take time — there are no quick fixes. The growing of opium in Afghanistan will fluctuate in quantity and has done so in the recent past.

A 2008 U.N. survey provided a very early indication of this year's possible cultivation levels. Compared to last year's good results, which showed a decline in production, this report indicates stable cultivation levels in the majority of Afghanistan's 31 provinces, an increase in cultivation in 13 provinces and a decrease in cultivation in three provinces. But as the independent drivers report produced for the FCO makes clear, it is misleading to focus only on headline figures as the wider picture is more complex. There is considerable diversity in cultivation and in the factors influencing farmers across the country.

The survey never assessed progress on implementation of

the eradication campaign, but stated only that eradication will be better organized in 2009 and is therefore expected to be more successful than in 2008. The current rise in poppy cultivation does not mean that progress is not being made in tackling the trade. Eradication is just part of the overall Afghan and international strategy to tackle poppy cultivation: large seizures are being made, the Afghan police are being trained, and alternative livelihoods are being created and counter narcotics institutions built up. Since the U.S. led invasion of Afghanistan in October 2001, the Golden Crescent opium trade has soared. According to the U.S. media, this lucrative contraband is protected by the Taliban, not to mention, of course, the regional warlords, in defiance of the "international community." The heroin business is said to be "filling the coffers of the Taliban." In the words of the U.S. State Department:

> Opium is a source of literally billions of dollars to extremist and criminal groups... Cutting down the opium supply is central to establishing a secure and stable democracy, as well as winning the global war on terrorism.
>
> Statement of Assistant Secretary of State Robert Charles, Congressional Hearing, April 1, 2004.

According to the United Nations Office on Drugs and Crime (UNODC), opium production in Afghanistan in 2008 as estimated at 6,000 tons, with an estimated area under cultivation of the order of 80,000 hectares. An even larger bumper harvest is predicted for 2008.The State Department suggests that up to 120,000 hectares were under cultivation in 2008. We could be on a path for a significant surge. Some observers indicate perhaps as much as 50 percent to 100 percent growth in the 2008 crop over the already troubling figures from last year. In response to the post-Taliban surge in opium production, the Bush administration has boosted its counter terrorism activities, while allocating substantial amounts of public money to the Drug Enforcement Administration's West Asia initiative, dubbed "Operation Containment." The various reports and official statements are, of course, blended in with the usual "balanced" self critique that "the international community is not doing enough" and that what we need is "transparency." Remarks on behalf of UNODC Executive Director at the U.N. General Assembly, October 2001:

> The headlines are "Drugs, warlords and insecurity overshadow Afghanistan's path to democracy." In chorus, the U.S. media is accusing the defunct "hard-line Islamic regime," without even acknowledging that the Taliban in collaboration with the United Nations - had imposed a successful ban on poppy cultivation in 2000. Opium production declined by more than 90 per cent in 2001.

In fact the surge in opium cultivation production coincided with the onslaught of the U.S.-led military operation and the downfall of the Taliban regime. From October through December 2001, farmers started to replant poppy on an extensive basis. The success of Afghanistan's 2000 drug eradication program under the Taliban had been acknowledged at the October 2001 session of the UN General Assembly (which took place barely a few days after the beginning of the 2001 bombing raids). No other UNODC member country was able to implement a comparable program:

> Turning first to drug control, I had expected to concentrate my remarks on the implications of the Taliban's ban on opium poppy cultivation in areas under their control...

We now have the results of our annual ground survey of poppy cultivation in Afghanistan. This year's production (2001) is around 185 tons. This is down from the 3300 tons last year (2000), a decrease of over 94 per cent. Compared to the record harvest of 4700 tons two years ago, the decrease is well over 97 per cent. Any decrease in illicit cultivation is welcomed, especially in cases like this when no displacement, locally or in other countries, took place to weaken the achievement.

In the wake of the U.S. invasion, there was a shift in rhetoric. UNODC is now acting as if the 2000 opium ban had never happened:

> ... The battle against narcotics cultivation has been fought and won in other countries and it [is] possible to do so here (in Afghanistan), with strong, democratic governance, international assistance and improved security and integrity.

> Statement of the UNODC Representative in Afghanistan at the February 2004 International Counter Narcotics Conference.

In fact, both Washington and the UNODC now claim that the objective of the Taliban in 2000 was not really "drug eradication," but a devious scheme to trigger "an artificial shortfall in supply," which would drive up World prices of heroin. Ironically, this twisted logic, which now forms part of a new "U.N. consensus," is refuted by a report of the UNODC office in Pakistan, which confirmed, at the time, that there was no evidence of stockpiling by the Taliban.

Desert News, Salt Lake City, Utah October 5, 2003.

In the wake of the 2001 U.S. bombing of Afghanistan, the British government of Tony Blair was entrusted by the G-8 Group of leading industrial nations to carry out a drug eradication program, which would, in theory, allow Afghan farmers to switch out of poppy cultivation into alternative crops. The British were working out of Kabul in close liaison with the U.S. DEA's "Operation Containment."

The U.K. sponsored crop eradication program is an obvious smokescreen. Since October 2001, opium poppy cultivation has skyrocketed. One of the "hidden" objectives of the war was precisely to restore the CIA sponsored drug trade to its historical levels and exert direct control over the drug routes. Immediately following the October 2001 invasion, opium markets were restored. Opium prices spiraled upwards. By early 2009, the opium price (in dollars/kg) was almost 15 times higher than in 2000. In 2001, under the Taliban, opiate production stood at 185 tons, increasing to 3400 tons in 2002 under the U.S. sponsored puppet regime of President Hamid Karzai. While highlighting Karzai's patriotic struggle against the Taliban, the media failed to mention that Karzai had actually collaborated with the Taliban. He had also been on the payroll of a major U.S. oil company, UNOCAL. In fact, since the mid-1990s, Hamid Karzai had acted as a consultant and lobbyist for UNOCAL in negotiations with the Taliban. According to the Saudi newspaper *Al-Watan*:

> Karzai has been a Central Intelligence Agency covert operator since the 1980s, funneling U.S. aid to the Taliban as of 1994 when the Americans had secretly and through the Pakistanis (specifically the 1SI) supported the Taliban's assumption of power.

It is worth recalling the history of the Golden Crescent drug trade, which is intimately related to the CIA's covert operations in the region since the onslaught of the Soviet-Afghan war and its aftermath. Prior to the Soviet-Afghan war (1979-1989), opium production in Afghanistan and Pakistan was directed to small regional markets. There was no local production of heroin. The Afghan narcotics economy was a carefully designed project of the CIA, supported by U.S. foreign policy. As revealed in the Iran-Contra and Bank of Commerce and Credit International (BCCI) scandals, CIA covert operations in support of the Afghan Mujahideen had been funded through the laundering of drug money. "Dirty money" was recycled through a number of banking institutions (in the Middle East) as well as through anonymous CIA shell companies, into "covert money," used to finance various insurgent groups during the Soviet- Afghan war, and its aftermath. Because the U.S. wanted to supply the Mujahideen rebels in Afghanistan with Stinger anti- aircraft missiles and other military hardware, it needed the full cooperation of Pakistan. By the mid-1980s, the CIA operation in Islamabad was one of the largest U.S. intelligence stations in the World.

> "If BCCI is such an embarrassment to the U.S. that forthright investigations are not being pursued it has a lot to do with the blind eye the U.S. turned to the heroin trafficking in Pakistan," said a U.S. intelligence officer.

Researcher Alfred McCoy's study confirms that within two years of the onslaught of the CIA's covert operation in Afghanistan in 1979, that the Pakistan-Afghanistan borderlands became the world's top heroin producer, supplying 60 per cent of U.S. demand. In Pakistan, the heroin-addict population went from near zero in 1979 to 1.2 million by 1985, a much steeper rise than in any other nation CIA assets again controlled this heroin trade. As the Mujahideen guerrillas seized territory inside Afghanistan, they ordered peasants to plant opium as a revolutionary tax. Across the border in Pakistan, Afghan leaders and local syndicates under the protection of Pakistan Intelligence operated hundreds of heroin laboratories. During this decade of wide-open drug-dealing, the U.S. Drug Enforcement Agency in Islamabad failed to instigate even one major seizure or arrest.

U.S. officials had refused to investigate charges of heroin dealing by its Afghan allies because U.S. narcotics policy in Afghanistan has been subordinated to the priorities of the war against Soviet influence there. In 1995, the former CIA director of the Afghan operation, Charles Cogan, admitted the CIA had indeed sacrificed the drug war to fight the Cold War:

> Our main mission was to do as much damage as possible to the Soviets. We didn't really have the resources or the time to devote to an investigation of the drug trade.
>
> I don't think that we need to apologize for this. Every situation has its fallout. There was fallout in terms of drugs, yes. But the main objective was accomplished. The Soviets left Afghanistan.

The role of the CIA, which is amply documented, is not mentioned in official UNODC publications, which focus on internal social and political factors. Needless to say, the historical roots of the opium trade have been grossly distorted. According to the UNODC, Afghanistan's opium production has increased more than 15-fold since 1979. In the wake of the Soviet-Afghan War, the growth of the narcotics economy has continued unabated. The Taliban, supported by the U.S., were initially instrumental in the further growth of opiate production until the 2000 opium ban. This recycling of drug money was used to finance the post-Cold War insurgencies in Central Asia and the Balkans including al-Qaeda. For details, see Michel Chossudovsky, War and Globalization, The Truth behind September 11, Global Outlook, 2002.

Narcotics: Second to Oil and the Arms Trade

The revenues generated from the CIA sponsored Afghan drug trade are sizeable. The Afghan trade in opiates constitutes a large share of the worldwide annual turnover of narcotics, which was estimated by the United Nations to be of the order of $400- 500 billion. At the time these U.N. figures were first brought out (1994), the (estimated) global trade in drugs was of the same order of magnitude as the global trade in oil.

The IMF estimated global money laundering to be between 590 billion and 1.5 trillion dollars a year, representing 2-5 percent of global GDP. (*Asian Banker,* August 15, 2003.) A large share of global money laundering as estimated by the IMF is linked to the trade in narcotics. Based on 2003 figures, drug trafficking constitutes "the third biggest global commodity in cash terms after oil and the arms trade." *The Independent,* February 29, 2004.

Moreover, the above figures including those on money laundering, confirm that the bulk of the revenues associated with the global trade in narcotics are not appropriated by terrorist groups and warlords, as suggested by the UNODC report. There are powerful business and financial interests behind narcotics. From this standpoint, geopolitical and military control over the drug routes is as strategic as oil and oil pipelines. However, what distinguishes narcotics from legal commodity trade is that narcotics constitute a major source of wealth formation not only for organized crime, but also for the U.S. intelligence apparatus, which increasingly constitutes a powerful actor in the spheres of finance and banking. In turn, the CIA, which protects the drug trade, has developed complex business and undercover links to major criminal syndicates involved in the drug trade. In other words, intelligence agencies and powerful business syndicates allied with organized crime are competing for the strategic control over the heroin routes. The multi-billion dollar revenues of narcotics are deposited in the Western banking system.

Most of the large international banks together with their affiliates in the offshore banking havens launder large amounts of narcotics-dollars. This trade can only prosper if the main actors involved in narcotics have "political friends in high places."

Legal and illegal undertakings are increasingly intertwined; the dividing line between "businesspeople" and criminals is blurred. In turn, the relationship among criminals, politicians and members of the intelligence establishment has tainted the structures of the state and the role of its institutions. This trade is characterized by a complex web of intermediaries. There are various stages of the drug trade, several interlocked markets, from the impoverished poppy farmer in Afghanistan to the wholesale and retail heroin markets in Western countries. In other words, there is a "hierarchy of price control" for opiates.

This hierarchy is acknowledged by the U.S. administration:

> Afghan heroin sells on the international narcotics market for 100 times the price farmers get for their opium right out of the field.
>
> U.S. State Department quoted by the *Voice of America.*

According to the UNODC, opium in Afghanistan generated in 2003 ... an income of one billion U.S. dollars for farmers and U.S. $1.3 billion for traffickers, equivalent to over half of its national income. Consistent with these UNODC estimates, the average price for fresh opium was $350 a kg. (2002); the 2002 production was 3400 tons. UNDOC estimates, based on local farm and wholesale prices constitute, however, a very small percentage of the total turnover of the multibillion dollar Afghan drug trade. The UNODC estimates "the total annual turn-over of international trade" in Afghan opiates at U.S. $30 billion. An examination of the wholesale and retail prices for heroin in the Western countries suggests, however, that the total revenues generated, including those at the retail level, are substantially higher. It is estimated that one kilo of opium produces approximately 100 grams of (pure) heroin.

The U.S. DEA confirms that SWA (South West Asia meaning Afghanistan) heroin in New York City was selling in the late 1990s for $85,000 to $190,000 per kilogram wholesale with a 75 percent purity ratio Since these figures were issued, sources say the prices for heroin have shown a growth of 450%.

According to the U.S. Drug Enforcement Administration (DEA) "the price of SEA (South East Asian) heroin ranges from $70,000 to $100,000 per unit (700 grams) and the purity of SEA heroin ranged from 85 to 90 percent." The SEA unit of 700 grams (85-90 % purity) translates into a wholesale price per kg. for pure heroin ranging between $115,000 and $163,000. The DEA figures quoted while reflecting the situation in the 1990s are broadly consistent with 2002 British figures. According to a report published in the *Guardian* (August 11, 2002), the wholesale price of (pure) heroin in London (U.K.) was of the order of 50,000 pounds sterling, approximately $80,000 (2002). Whereas, as there is competition between different sources of heroin supply, it should be emphasized that Afghan heroin represents a rather small percentage of the U.S. heroin market, which is largely supplied out of Colombia.

The New York Police Department (NYPD) notes that retail heroin prices are down and purity is relatively high. Heroin previously sold for about $90 per gram but now sells for $65 to $70 per gram or less. Anecdotal information from the NYPD indicates that purity for a bag of heroin commonly ranges from 50 to 80 percent but can be as low as 30 percent. Information as of June 2008 indicates that bundles (10 bags) purchased by Dominican buyers from Dominican sellers in larger quantities (about 150 bundles) sold for as little as $40 each, or $55 each in Central Park. The DEA reports that an ounce of heroin usually sells for $2,500 to $5,000, a gram for $70 to $95, a bundle for $80 to $90, and a bag for $10.

The DMP reports that the average heroin purity at the street level in 1999 was about 62 percent. The NYPD and DEA retail price figures seem consistent. The DEA price of $70-$95, with a purity of 62 percent translates into $112 to $153 per gram of pure heroin. The NYPD figures are roughly similar with perhaps lower estimates for purity. It should be noted that when heroin is purchased in very small quantities, the retail price tends to be much higher. In the U.S., purchase is often by "the bag" (the typical bag contains 25 milligrams of pure heroin). A $10 dollar bag in NYC (according to the DEA figure quoted above) would convert into a price of $400 per gram, each bag containing 0.025gr. of pure heroin. In other words, for very small purchases marketed by street pushers, the retail margin tends to be significantly higher. In the case of the $10 bag purchase, it is roughly 3 to 4 times the corresponding retail price per gram ($112-$153). In Britain, the retail street price per gram of heroin, according to British Police sources, "... fell from £74 in 1997 to £61 (in 2004)." (I.e. from approximately $133 to $110, based on the 2004 rate of exchange) Independent, March 3, 2004.

In some cities it was as low as £30-40 per gram with a low level of purity, the average price for a gram of heroin in Britain is between £40 and £90 ($72-$ 162 per gram). (The report does not mention purity.) The street price of heroin was £80 per gram in April 2007 according to the National Criminal Intelligence Service. We are dealing with prices, from the farm price in the producing country, upwards, to the final retail street price. The latter is often 80-100 times the price paid to the farmer. In other words, the opiate product transits through several markets from the producing country to the trans-shipment countries, to the consuming countries. In the latter, there are wide margins between "the landing price" at the point of entry, demanded by the drug cartels and the wholesale prices and the retail street prices, protected by Western organized crime. In Afghanistan, the reported production of 3600 tons of opium in 2003 would allow for the production of approximately 360,000 kg of pure heroin. Gross revenues accruing to Afghan farmers are roughly estimated by the UNODC to be of the order of $1 billion, with 1.3 billion accruing to local traffickers. When sold in Western markets at a heroin wholesale price of the order of $100,000 a kg (with a 70 percent purity ratio), the global wholesale proceeds (corresponding to 3600 tons of Afghan opium) would be of the order of $51.4 billion dollars.

The latter constitutes a conservative estimate based on the various figures for wholesale prices in the previous section. The total proceeds of the Afghan narcotics trade (in terms of total value added) is estimated using the final heroin retail price. In other words, the retail value of the trade is ultimately the criterion for measuring the importance of the drug trade in terms of revenue generation and wealth formation. A meaningful estimate of the retail value, however, is almost impossible to ascertain due to the fact that retail prices vary considerably within urban areas, from one city to another and between consuming countries, not to mention variations in purity and quality. The evidence on retail margins, namely the difference between wholesale and retail values in the consuming countries, nonetheless, suggests that a large share of the total (money) proceeds of the drug trade are generated at the retail level. In other words, a significant portion of the proceeds of the drug trade accrues to criminal and business syndicates in Western countries involved in the local wholesale and retail narcotics markets. And the various criminal gangs involved in retail trade are invariably protected by "Corporate" Crime Syndicates.

90 percent of heroin consumed in the U.K. is from Afghanistan. Using the British retail price figure from U.K. police sources of $110 a gram (with an assumed 50 percent purity level), the total retail value of the Afghan narcotics trade in 2003 (3600 tons of opium) would be on the order of 79.2 billion dollars. The latter should be considered as a simulation rather than an estimate. Under this assumption (simulation), a billion dollars gross revenue to the farmers

in Afghanistan (2003) would generate global narcotics earnings — accruing at various stages and in various markets — of the order of 79.2 billion dollars.

These global proceeds accrue to business syndicates, intelligence agencies, organized crime, financial institutions, wholesalers, retailers, etc., involved directly or indirectly in the drug trade. In turn, the proceeds of this lucrative trade are deposited in Western banks, which constitute an essential mechanism in the laundering of dirty money. A very small percentage accrues to farmers and traders in the producing country. Bear in mind that the net income accruing to Afghan farmers is but a fraction of the estimated 1 billion dollar amount. The latter does not include payments of farm inputs, interest on loans to money lenders, political protection, etc. Afghanistan produces over 70 percent of the global supply of heroin and heroin represents a sizeable fraction of the global narcotics market, estimated by the U.N. to be of the order of $400-500 billion.

There are no reliable estimates on the distribution of the global narcotics trade between the main categories:

- ➤ Cocaine, Opium/Heroin,
- ➤ Cannabis, Amphetamine Type Stimulants (ATS),
- ➤ Other Drugs.

The proceeds of the drug trade are deposited in the normal banking system. Drug money is laundered in the numerous offshore banking havens in Switzerland, Luxembourg, the British Channel Islands, the Cayman Islands and some 50 other locations around the globe. It is here that the criminal syndicates involved in the drug trade and the representatives of the world's largest commercial banks interact. Dirty money is deposited in these offshore havens, which are controlled by the major Western commercial banks. The latter have a vested interest in maintaining and sustaining the drug trade.

Once the money has been laundered, it can be recycled into bona fide investments not only in real estate, hotels, etc., but also in other areas such as the services economy and manufacturing. Dirty and covert money is also funneled into various financial instruments including the trade in derivatives, primary commodities, stocks, and government bonds. U.S. foreign policy supports the workings of a thriving criminal economy in which the demarcation between organized capital and organized crime has become increasingly blurred.

The heroin business is not "filling the coffers of the Taliban" as claimed by U.S. Government and the international community: quite the opposite! The proceeds of this illegal trade are the source of wealth formation, largely reaped by powerful business/criminal interests within the Western countries.

These interests are sustained by U.S. foreign policy. Decision- making in the U.S. State Department, the CIA and the Pentagon is instrumental in supporting this highly profitable multibillion dollar trade, third in commodity value after oil and the arms trade.

The Afghan drug economy is "protected." The heroin trade was part of the war agenda. What this war has achieved is to restore a compliant narcotic-state, headed by a U.S. appointed puppet.

The powerful financial interests behind narcotics are supported by the militarization of the world's major drug triangles (and trans-shipment routes), including the Golden Crescent and the Andean region of South America (under the so-called Andean Initiative).

Opium Poppy Cultivation in Afghanistan

Year	Production (in tons)	Cultivation (in hectares)
1994	71,470	3,400
1995	53,759	2,300
1996	56,824	2,200
1997	58,416	2,800
1998	63,674	2,700
1999	90,983	4,600
2000	82,172	3,300
2001	7,606	185
2002	74,000	3,400
2007	88,000	4,000

Chapter Three

The Phony Drug War

I n the history of all nations there is a clearly defined point when a marked decline leading to its inevitable downfall is traceable. This is true of India, even as far back as the Harrapa culture; the invasion of India and the great Aryan cultures set up there by the Scythians and the Hellenics under Alexander the Great. The principle cultural changes that ruined civilizations in Europe came from four main routes.

> ➢ From Western Asia through Russia to central and Western Europe.

> ➢ From Asia Minor through the Aegean by sea to the Western Mediterranean.

> ➢ From the Near East and the Aegean by sea to the Western Mediterranean.

> ➢ From North Africa to Spain and Western Europe.

Both the Greek and Roman civilizations were brought down by these currents or a combination thereof. It is certain that the wholesale movement of people and the spread of various cultures played a major role in shaping the future of nations. That such mass movements were induced by trade and political reasons is clearly recorded. Strange people and strange cultures began to demand "rights" in ancient Rome.

The decadent among the Roman rulers for political reasons acquiesced to the demands. Nowhere can this current of mass movement of people for political gain be more clearly traced than in the history of the United States of America. In 1933, President Franklin Delano Roosevelt opened wide the floodgates of an invasion of Eastern European people whose culture was utterly alien to the Christian Anglo Saxon, Nordic Alpine, Lombardy Germanic culture that comprised the mass of the people of the United States. He did this purely for political purposes knowing that the alien immigrants would vote for him and his party.

This vast tidal wave of socially and culturally unassimilated people came about as a result of political decisions taken by the Conspirators whose goal was to wreck Christian America. That policy continues today. The United States is being swamped by alien peoples from Asia Minor, the Far East, the Near East, the Pacific Islands, Eastern Europe, Central and South America, to such an extent that is safe to say the decline and fall of the United States, begun in 1933 is now well into its stride.

Cultural changes have been vast, especially since 1933. Under the guise of "tolerance" and "internationalism," the Western Christian population of the United States has been forced to retreat before the pressures of "liberalism." Compromise became the order of the day. The White Christian ethic which once abounded in the United States began drowning in a sea of non- Christian ideas, which if left unchecked will, in a comparatively short time, do to the United States what was done to Rome.

One of the most fiendish efforts to destroy the Western Christian ethic of what I call the indigenous people of America, that is, those White Christians, whose forbears came from England, Ireland, Scotland, Wales, Germany, Scandinavia, France and Italy, was the cultural havoc brought about through rock and roll music accompanied by the wholesale use of habit-forming drugs, such as marijuana, chemical substances, heroin and cocaine. We should never allow ourselves to fall into the trap of thinking that somehow these disastrous cultural changes just happened. Happenstance does not play a role in this narrative. Here we deal with facts, and the fact is that the whole vast cultural shift from Christian morality to pagan decadence was carefully planned.

In the many works that I have written, these plans are laid bare, and the names provided of the institutions, companies, organizations and individuals who are responsible for the terrible war on White Christian America. Among my works are the following:

> ➢ Institutions and Companies of the Conspirators.
> ➢ Black Nobility Unmasked.
> ➢ Who Are The Conspirators?
> ➢ Hidden Rulers of America.
> ➢ New Age of Aquarius.

This is by no means all that I have done to disclose the menace of drugs. Throughout all of my more than five hundred monographs and audio tapes, mention is made of this insidious trade and who is behind it. Drawing upon their vast experience and wealth obtained from the China opium trade of the 18th and 19th centuries, the British oligarchist families and their American cousins began their onslaught on the drug front in earnest against America immediately following the Second World War. I remind you that the research work for my personal war on drugs was conducted mainly on location and that my information is drawn from intelligence and ex-intelligence connections involved in monitoring the drug trade in a number of countries.

Back in the 1930s, a certain authority on British investment abroad, a Mr. Graham, wrote that British investment in Latin America amounted to "in excess of 1 trillion pounds." Why so much money in Latin America? In a word; drugs. It certainly wasn't bananas; although that fruit did indeed play a role in covering shipments of drugs hidden under bunches of bananas.

The plutocracy holding bank purse strings then is the same as those who are in the drug trade today. No one will ever catch the nobility of England with dirty hands; they have their respectable facades behind which they operate through front men and organizations like Frasers in Africa, and Trinidad Leaseholds Ltd. in the Caribbean (large British companies registered in London).

During Queen Victoria's reign, fifteen members of parliament in England controlled the vast trade in China and Latin America, and they included Lord Chamberlain, Sir Charles Barry and Lord Palmerston. Just as the China opium trade was a British monopoly, the drug trade in the Caribbean, Central and South America, the Middle and Far East, became a British monopoly.

Later, in pursuance of their aims to destroy America culturally, some of the old "blue blood" families of America were allowed into the trade; Thomas Handiside Perkins, the Delanos and the Richardsons are examples of what I mean. Starting with distribution by "missionaries" of the China

Inland Mission, heavily funded by the BEIC, opium was forced upon the Chinese population. The demand was created and then met through the BEIC.

Their servant, Adam Smith classified it "Free Trade." When the Chinese government attempted to resist their people being turned into opium addicts, Britain fought two major wars to stop what it called "interference in free trade."

While I was studying in London, I met the son of a missionary family who had served with the China Inland Mission. His family had been missionaries since the 19th Century. After a fairly close friendship with one of the daughters who had also served in China, she confided in me that they all smoked opium, and that it was a tradition that had been in their family for generations.

The Indo-China opium trade is one of the best-kept secrets and one of the most dastardly chapters in Western European history. We must remember that the British royal family has its origins in Venice, that Levantine dagger in the heart of Western Europe. Robert Bruce, who usurped the throne of Scotland, came from Venice and his real name was not Bruce. The same could be said of the so-called "House of Windsor," in reality The House of Black Guelphs.

As previously mentioned, following their success in India and China, the BEIC turned its attention to the United States, which is one of the reasons why we have a so-called "special relationship" with the British aristocracy, and indeed, many of our "leaders" are related to British royalty. Franklin D. Roosevelt and George Herbert Walker Bush and Richard Cheney are examples that come to mind. The lucrative drug trade established in China is one of the worst examples of making huge sums of money out of human misery.

Under the protection of the Swiss government's Industrial Espionage Act, freely invoked, provides for severe prison sentences, if anything is disclosed about the actions of these two companies, or indeed about any Swiss companies. Do not rock the Swiss boat unless you are not prepared for some very unpleasant consequences! Rhetoric by people like Mrs. Thatcher and George Bush who tell us in ringing tones that they are committed to fighting a drug war may be completely disregarded.

The so-called "war on drugs" is absolutely phony at higher levels of government. There is no drug war going on, and there never has been. Not until the British and American governments go after the people at the top of the drug trade will their proclaimed "war" make sense. This means arresting people like the Keswicks, the Jardines, the Mathesons and closing banks like the Midland Bank, the National and Westminster Bank, Barclays and the Royal Bank of Canada. I do not mention these names of British upper-crust establishment lightly.

As far back as 1931, the heads of these companies and banks were made peers of the realm. It was the Queen of England herself who extended special protection to the big five drug trade companies in England. Through my trusted friend, I was given sight of the papers of the late Frederick Wells Williamson, trustee of the India Papers. What I saw shocked me. The list of "noble" families in England and Europe involved in the drug trade would cause a storm of indignation to sweep Britain and Europe if ever the crowned vipers were to be revealed.

Following the Second World War, a flood of heroin threatened to engulf the Western world, with particular attention directed to North America. The trade was run and financed by the very top people. The KGB used it as a weapon against the West under the orders and direction of the late Yuri Andropov. Supplied and financed by the KGB, facilities to make cocaine and heroin were established in Cuba, under the direction of Raoul Castro, brother of Fidel Castro.

These facts are known to the United States Government, which was never able to do anything to put the Cuban facilities out of business and the policies appear to leave Cuba "untouchable." Galen, the noted authority on heroin should be read by all who desire to have a clear understanding of what heroin is and what it does to the human body. Probably the first recorded users of opium (from which heroin is derived) were the ancient Moguls of India, whose dynasty lasted from 1526 to 1858 and whose civilization crumbled commensurate with the production of opium and increased British power.

A map of India which I acquired from the India Papers, India House, London show areas where the opium poppy was grown, and is commensurate with acquisition of territory by the British starting from 1785, all along the Ganges Basin, Bihar and Benares. The finest quality opium came from poppies grown in these areas. It is just awesome what the British opium lords, that is to say, the ruling British establishment in England were able to accomplish in India.

The royalty and their hangers-on called this fantastically lucrative trade "the spoils of the Empire." The papers of India House, called "Miscellaneous Old Records" proved to be a treasure house of information for me. The papers show the total involvement of the top people in the British government, royalty and the oligarchy, in the China opium trade.

These records show that "instant fortunes" were made by the "nobility" and "aristocracy" of Britain. Outsiders, like one William Sullivan, who was put on trial for making an unauthorized "instant fortune" for himself at the expense of the British East India Company, soon found themselves in deep trouble. The British East India Company directors were top members of the Conservative Party, including Lord Palmerston et al. They belonged to the best gentlemen's clubs in London. They had their own British East India Company passports, which became necessary if one wanted to visit China.

The lords and ladies who owned the British East India Company first tried in 1683 to introduce opium into England, but the sturdy yeoman and middle class could not be induced to become dope addicts. So the plutocrats and oligarchy began casting around for a market.

The Arabian Peninsula was tried, but that also failed, thanks to the teachings of the prophet Mohammed. And so they turned to China with its teeming masses, so conveniently close to Bengal. It was not until 1729 that the Chinese government tried to pass anti-opium laws, and that put China on a collision course with Britain. British aristocracy and its oligarchist structure are very hard to penetrate. For persons without special training, such a task is impossible. The vast majority of British political leaders of any importance are related to each other, with so-called titles being taken over by the eldest son on the death of the senior member of the family, and virtually all of these families are in the drug trade, indirectly of course.

Perhaps you may find this detail somewhat tedious. I know I found it so when I was reading through mountains of documents in London, and recording the information in my stock of notebooks. Where I was not permitted to make such notes, my special "spy" camera served me well. I am providing this information, which took a great deal of research, because it profoundly affects the United States of America.

It is part of the "special relationship" cover-up tying our own "noble families" of the drug trade to their British "cousins." This "special relationship" has camouflaged a nasty situation where an alien element that crept into British aristocracy was inherited by their American cousins.

Take the case of Lord Halifax, Britain's Ambassador to Washington, who to all intents and purposes took control of U.S. foreign policy prior to and during the Second World War, including oversight of all U.S. intelligence capabilities. His son, Charles Wood married a Miss Primrose, a blood relative of the horrible and ignoble House of Rothschild, with names like Lord Swayling and Montague associated with Queen Elizabeth the co- majority stockholder of the Shell Company. I tie all of these people and their institutions to the drug trade.

One of the ancestors of this brood was Lord Palmerston, perhaps one of the most respected British Prime Ministers of all times. He also just happened to be the prime mover in the China opium trade. These "crowned vipers" allowed their British "cousins" in America to get in on the trade when they needed to move large opium stocks to the interior of China. Chinese Commissioner Un, noted:

> There is so much opium on board the English vessels now

lying in the roads, (Macao) which will never be returned to the country from which it came. A sale must be made here on the coast and I shall not be surprised to hear of it being smuggled in (to China) under American colors.

Commissioner Un never lived long enough to discover just how accurate his forecast was and which led indirectly to drug the infestation of the United States. We must examine how we, the public, are bluffed and kept in the dark as to what is going on.

One thing we can be sure of; by the time this work is read, no one will be left in doubt that U.S. efforts to stem the flow of drugs to this country and end the drug trade, are fatally flawed, and that such flaws and failures are by design.

Our government does not want the drug trade to dry up. The powers that be, those who control "our" representatives in the Congress, have long ago decreed that any war against drugs shall be a mere show war. Two important members of government have resigned over this unwillingness to do anything at the top in the so-called war on drugs. An Attorney General was forced to resign because he was perceived to be in bed with the Mexican government, protecting them at the highest level. A President was forced out of office, because he dared to try and take on the top people in the drug trade. The British moved their opium trade from Canton to Hong Kong, and thence to Panama, which is why it was so important to get General Noriega out of the way, permanently.

Heroin flowed from Afghanistan through Pakistan via the desolate coast of Maccra across the Red Sea to Dubai, where it was traded for gold. It flowed from Lebanon, from the Bekka Valley, controlled by Syria, which is why Syria's armed forces occupied Lebanon for so long; it flowed from the Golden Triangle of Burma and Thailand, and from the Golden Crescent in Iran, which is why the Shah was first deposed and then murdered when he found out what was going on and attempted to end it.

This very real drug war against the United States is part of the One World Government conspiracy, a conspiracy that has its roots in the Committee of 300. The history of drugs is as old as the history of man himself. The conspiracy to overturn all existing governments and religions is a tripartite effort - spiritual, economic and political. Drugs are its main weapon. Gnosticism is the counterforce to Christianity. The Queen of England is a Gnostic as is her husband, Prince Philip. In this is found the free use of drugs, mother worship, the Earth Goddess, Theosophy and the Rosicrucians, who ran the Chinese Opium Gangs known as "Triads." The "Triads" obtained their supplies of opium from the British ship warehouses, and then forced Chinese property owners to open opium dens.

Alistair Crowley was the demon-dope role model in Victorian British society. Out of this came "rock and roll," via the Tavistock Institute that manufactured "rock groups" as vehicles for the spread of the use of LSD, marijuana and latterly, cocaine. We may not know it, but such decadent groups as "The Rolling Stones" enjoy the patronage of the top British families and the German oligarchy family of Von Thurn und Taxis. The venerated British noble families have long been in the drug business through the Hong Kong and Shanghai Bank, affectionately known as the "Hongshang Bank." The business of the Hong Kong and Shanghai Bank is drugs, plain and simple. From these noble families came the plot to assassinate Abraham Lincoln and later, John F. Kennedy. Their domination over the United

States is complete, acting through their institutions and companies, "cut-out" religious organizations. The Royal Family of England is the real owner of the Bronfman liquor empire.

At the time of Prohibition, The Bronfmans were the largest smugglers of bootleg alcohol from Canada into the U.S. Americans must never forget that these powerful men and their companies are responsible for the vast river of drugs in which America is literally drowning. Our leading control body is the Royal Institute for International Affairs (RIIA). The chairman of Morgan Guarantee is also on the board of the RIIA.

Other Morgan board members are on the board of the Hong Kong and Shanghai Bank.

Lord Cato appears on the "London Committee" of the Hong Kong and Shanghai Bank. It is the RIIA, through a network of companies, institutions and banks that is responsible for the worldwide drug menace. It was the RIIA that set Mao Tse Tung up in power in China, and then established Hong Kong as the number one opium and gold trading post in the world, a position it held until the recent expansion of Dubai. Some time ago I wrote about the Australian end of the dope trade and mentioned its methodology. I received a letter from a man who told me that he had been a courier for one the biggest money launderings outfits, and that my information was very accurate.

The Australian company was controlled out of England. I have previously mentioned the threat made by Chou En-Lai to President Nasser of Egypt. Both are deceased, but what the Chinese leader said is worth repeating:

Some of them (U.S. troops in Vietnam) are trying opium. We are helping them. Do you remember when the West (i.e. the British), imposed opium on us? They fought us with opium. And now we are going to fight them with their own weapons. The effect this demoralization will have on the United States will be far greater than anyone realizes.

This conversation was recorded in June of 1965 by Mohammed Heikel, the much-respected former editor of the Egyptian daily, "Al Ahram." Offshore banks that are known launderers of drug money and who are affiliated with the Royal Institute for International Affairs are scattered throughout the world. Here is a list of the countries where they are located:

Singapore	14
Bahamas	23
Antigua	5
Antilles	10
Bermuda	5
Trinidad	6
Caymans	22
Panama	30

This list excludes RIIA banks under Chinese control. For a list of these you can consult Polk's Banking Directory. The lists of names of prominent individuals would fill pages. Suffice to say that among them are the most prominent among British society, like Sir Mark Turner, who controls the British royal family's big banks, including the Royal Bank of Canada. It was Turner's antecedents who conspired with King George III to harm the American Colonists. The biggest opium-for-gold business is transacted in Dubai by the British Bank of the Middle East. The amount of gold traded in Dubai exceeds that sold in New York. This operation is in the hands of Sir Humphrey Trevelyn.

The world price of gold is "fixed" every day at the offices of N.M. Rothschild, St. Swithins Court, London. It is based solely upon the ruling price of opium. Those who meet in the offices of N. M. Rothschild are representatives of Harry Oppenheimer's Anglo American Company of South Africa, Moccato Metals, Johnson Matthey Kleinwart Benson, Sharps, Pixley Wardley, and members of the London Committee of the Hong Kong and Shanghai Bank.

Between them, these companies and their representatives reflect the controlling body of the opium-heroin trade, from the amount to be grown, the price to be paid and conversely, the price of gold; who shall trade; where; and in what amounts.

"Outsiders" who try to break in are quickly reported to David Rockefeller's private police network known as "Interpol," which sometime results in relative small quantities of drugs being seized. These are hailed by the world press as "major victories" in the phony drug war. The wholesale trade in heroin and cocaine is conducted through the following major banks. Thus far, no government has dared to go after them, although evidence of their nefarious activities abounds:

U.S.A.

➤ The Bank of Nova Scotia

➤ Harry Winston Diamond Dealers

- Mocatto Metals
- N.M.R. Metals
- Loeb Rhodes
- Engelhard Minerals
- Bank of Dadeland
- First Bank of Boston
- Credit Suisse

CANADA

- The Royal Bank of Canada
- Noranda Sales Corporation
- Canadian Imperial Bank
- Bank of Nova Scotia
- Hong Kong. Sharp Pixlee Wardley
- Inchcape Company
- Charter Consolidated
- Hong Kong and Shanghai Bank
- Standard and Chartered Bank
- Overseas Chinese Bank
- Jardine Matheson
- Sime, Darby
- Bangkok Bank MIDDLE EAST
- The British Bank of the Middle East
- Barclays International Bank, Dubai

- ➢ Barclays Discount Bank
- ➢ Israel Bank Leumi
- ➢ Bank Hapolum of India

PANAMA

- ➢ Bancoiberia America
- ➢ Banconacional de Panama

ENGLAND

- ➢ National Westminster Bank
- ➢ Midlands Bank
- ➢ Barclays Bank

Panama is important in the world of drugs, because it was set up as a trading area for cocaine. Major commercial banks were opened there for this purpose. Strongman Omar Torrijos was placed in charge, but when he switched affiliations, he was "terminated."

When General Noriega, acting according to a USDEA mandate he thought he had received, began ripping the lid off Rockefeller's drug banking empire in Panama, he was kidnapped by a 7,000 strong military contingent under the command of President G.W.H. Bush and brought to Miami to stand trial as a major "drug dealer." He paid the price by being "judicially" sentenced to prison from which he will never emerge.

President Nixon thought he was big enough to take on the heroin trade coming through France. He found out he was wrong and lost his Presidency because of his audacious attempt to upset the "special connection" between Britain and the U.S.

The "Corporation" always has on hand about 200 tons of cocaine paste, while it is an established fact that in his heyday, Pato Pizzaro ran hundreds of millions of dollars through Panamanian banks. Pizzarro was head of "The Corporation," a Bolivian entity, until he was murdered on orders of the Medellin Cartel for trying to "cut them out." One man who knew all about what was going on in Panama, but who did no reporting was Alfredo Duncan, the DEA agent-in- charge attached to the U.S. Embassy. Alfredo Duncan was primarily responsible for the escape of "The Corporations" money laundering man, Remberto, one of the most important money men in the Bolivian ring operating in Panama.

The ring was set up by David Rockefeller as the main cocaine banking depository just as the British had Hong Kong set up for heroin trading. Remberto was enticed to Panama. He waited around for a supposed deal to go through, but when Edwin Meese, then Attorney General reportedly warned the Mexican government of what was about to happen, Remberto was allowed to slip away, thus avoiding arrest. The agent in charge, Alfredo Duncan, received dozens of cables from the DEA in Washington ordering him to apprehend Remberto. When it was evident that the bird had flown the coop, DEA agent Alfredo Duncan blamed the CIA, saying that they "whisked him (Remberto) away to Contadora Island." Thus was thwarted what could have been a major triumph for the war on drugs. Instead it ended in a fiasco of blocked or disregarded orders. One is left with a net impression that Remberto was deliberately allowed to escape.

In the much vaunted and terribly costly "Operations Snowcap," the DEA was supposed to go into the Bolivian jungles and smash the huge cocaine laboratories. From the very start, "Operation Snowcap" was a fraudulent farce, intended it seems, to fool Congress and the American people into believing that the DEA was scoring great successes in this phony war. "Operation Snowcap" was like the Vietnam War. The United States has no intention of winning it. We dare not; the game is too big. This phony drug war is shot-through with deceit, lies, and hypocrisy. In short it is a waste of time and taxpayer's money, a cruel hoax, altogether meaningless. Just as the U.S. government was willing to sacrifice the lives of its servicemen in Vietnam, knowing all the while that we had no interest in defeating the enemy, thus was the government willing to sacrifice the lives of dedicated young DEA agents, several of whom died in the line of duty during "Operation Snowcap."

Lt. Colonel Oliver North has long been suspect in the opinion of a member of the U.S. Senate. The information I have about his actions in blowing a drug operation in Colombia, leads me to believe even more firmly that our government had no intention of winning its much advertised "drug war."

In many of my monographs on drugs, I wrote extensively about the Medellin Cartel and the Colombian cocaine barons. In this regard, at the risk of "advertising," I am going to say that I was in the vanguard of disclosing the name "Medellin Cartel" and the whole Colombian cocaine trade in general.

Contrary to popular belief, the bulk of cocaine is not processed in Colombia, but comes from Bolivia. Official

DEA Custom's figures show that ninety seven percent of all cocaine originates in Bolivia. The reason why Colombia gets all the limelight is because the Bolivians are not a violent people, nor do they hardly ever leave Bolivia to deal. If one wants to buy cocaine, one has to travel to Bolivia.

In the case involving Oliver North, Bobby Seale, a deep cover agent who had penetrated the Medellin cartel, believed that the Medellin Cartel was actually bribing Daniel Ortega, head of the Sandinista. He turned the information over to the DEA and they gave it to North. It provided North with a golden chance to back up his glowing words with deeds. Instead, he chose to doubt the information provided by Seale, whom history will show was the most effective undercover DEA officer ever in place in Colombia. North then told the DEA he wanted Seale to ferry cash to the Contras.

I could never imagine why North would want to remove Seale from his dynamic role; here was a man who was really fighting a drug war for our side. When Seale refused to be seconded to North, he leaked the Seale story to the press. What was the outcome? Possibly the best operation ever mounted by the DEA was destroyed and Seale was murdered by Medellin Cartel hit men, after being stripped of protection and his address made public through a judge's order. You don't believe me? Since my expose, a full length movie was made in which the story is portrayed exactly as I set it out 4 years before Seale was murdered. It is not my wish to sit in judgment upon Lt. Colonel North, but leaking the Seale story to the jackals of the American media ranks in treachery to the way in which the New York Times leaked our satellite codes to the Soviet Union via one of its reporters, Richard Burt. At the very least, North has a lot of explaining to do. In my view North ranks only one step above a "dirt bag," street slang for an informer. A very serious loss was incurred by the death of Bobby Seale. But for the Iran-Contra hearings, this deplorable occurrence would probably have gone unreported.

In my view, the North "leak" was no accident and certainly not an isolated incident. This is not the only time evidence has emerged that our government is not fully at war against drugs. In another Colombian case involving the Medellin Cartel, one of its top Bolivian suppliers, Roberto Suarez lost 850 pounds of cocaine and two of his top drug henchmen who were arrested in a Miami bust. Suarez had an income of $1 million a day, and it was steady income at this level. He was more of the ruler of Bolivia than its President.

High-level government figures in Latin America showed up repeatedly in documentation for this case. Shortly after the arrest of two top Suarez "drug diplomats," the most terrifying coup was launched against the Bolivian government, which was backed by the DEA and the CIA. The coup succeeded, and cost the lives of thousands of people and ended with Bolivia becoming the principal cocaine supplier for Colombia. Perhaps this is why charges against the two Suarez "drug diplomats" arrested in Miami were dropped and bail mysteriously lowered for the third man, thereby enabling them to fly home the same day.

Now remember, these were not your average NBC Nightly News small time dealers. These men were at the very top of the drug cartel, so it was not a problem to put up the lesser amount of bail money and leave the U.S. Was this only a coincidence? Those who have unwarranted faith in our government and our President may like to believe it wasn't anything but an accident, but with hundreds of similar cases going wrong, how can we trust our government? Apparently I am not alone in my suspicions. Former Customs Commissioner William von Raab once said that his department was more interested in pursuing cases of parrot smuggling than going after the big time drug dealers.

Von Raab was the target of Congressional venom when he denounced the entire Mexican government as corrupt. Facts and circumstances appear to give strong backing to Von Raabs grievous charges. Mexico responds routinely to charges that its highest officials are up to their hocks in the drug trade by saying "give us proof so that we can investigate your charges." Every time an opportunity arises to provide proof, mysterious forces inside our government step in and thwart the action.

One such case involved a certain Hector Alvares, a member of the press corps of former President Salinas de Goltari. Alvares and another front man, Pablo Giron, told a DEA deep cover agent posing as a big buyer of cocaine, that he could make arrangements with the Mexican government to ferry shipments of Bolivian cocaine destined for the U.S. through Mexico. This was during the preliminary discussions of a "buy" of Bolivian cocaine base. Giron said he had a direct line to Mexican General Poblana Silvo, who would act on his (Giron's) phone call.

Giron told a DEA agent (who has sworn to this) that he was very close to Salinas de Gottari. A Customs informant also swore to being told that Alvarez was in a Secret Service detail to protect President-elect Goltari. In that particular proposed "buy," sixteen tons of cocaine was involved. This was totally separate from "Operation Snowcap." During the discussions in Panama, Alfredo Duncan, the DEA agent in charge in Panama, let it be known to a number of DEA agents and Customs agents that General Manuel Noriega was "a DEA man." This was confirmed at least three times in letters from John Lawn, head of the DEA in Washington.

Two others involved with Alvarez were the Bolivians Ramon and Vargas, who owned a cocaine laboratory in Bolivia that regularly produced 200 kilos of cocaine per month. Eventually, the DEA agent "buyer," a contract pilot and a customs agent, gained the confidence of the Bolivians and were invited to inspect their facilities deep in the Bolivian jungles. What they found left them staggering drunk with amazement.

They discovered seven airstrips fully capable of handling 747s, next to very large underground laboratories and support buildings, an amazing complex, guarded by heavily armed troops. The transaction they were involved in called for the purchase of 5000 tons of cocaine. Yet in all of the years that "Snowcap" had been operating, the DEA had come nowhere near to getting even close to the Bolivian facilities.

When the deep cover agent asked Ramon and Vargas if they were not afraid of "Operation Snowcap," they simply laughed. Ramon and Vargas had good reason to be filled with mirth. "Operation Snowcap" was a bureaucratic nightmare. All the wrong equipment was sent to Bolivia, most of it useless, and a lot more "bungles" Vargas said. No one in Bolivia was in the least bit concerned about "Operation Snowcap." The aircraft allotted to "Snowcap" did not have the range needed to reach the jungle facilities and the few helicopters were completely inadequate for the job. Was this just another of many "bungles?"

I do not believe it was simply a bureaucratic bungle. From information I gleaned, it would appear that these "mistakes" were deliberate sabotage. For one thing, the firepower of the DEA agents could not hope to match the military-style capabilities of "the Corporation."

In 1988 the DEA spent one hundred million dollars on "Operation Snowcap." What did we get for it? About fifteen thousand kilos of cocaine and partly processed cocaine!

Now, while this may sound like a lot, when measured against the production capacities of "The Corporation," it was a mere drop in the ocean. Remember, the fifteen thousand kilos represented less than 3 months of Bolivian production of cocaine. Why didn't we just go out and buy the cocaine at a far cheaper price -- which we could have done — as the deep cover agent had begged everyone in Washington to be allowed to do?

The answer is that the DEA refused to put up the money for a buy that would not only have netted a huge amount of fully processed cocaine, but also four of the Bolivian "The Corporation's" top executive officers. It would also have provided the United States with the proof it heretofore lacked of Mexican government involvement at the highest level.

➢ Why did the DEA refuse to put up the money?

➢ Why did the Assistant U.S. Attorney in San Diego refuse to grant a wiretap, which would have snared Mexican General Poblano Silva, whom Giron was about to call on the phone and implicate in a massive cocaine buy?

➢ Why did Attorney General Edwin Meese get on the

phone to the Mexican Attorney General and warn him of the coming DEA operation that would have resulted in General Poblano Silva being implicated in a major Bolivian cocaine distribution plot?

➢ Customs Commissioner William von Raab is said to have resigned in disgust over the Meese telephone warning - And what of our "drug war" in Colombia?

How has the U.S. fared there? The answer is that we have fared far worse in Colombia than anywhere else on Earth, in spite of pouring millions of dollars into the "drug war" in that country alone. President G.H.W. Bush did not do anything of significance in Colombia. On February 25, 1991, Colombian President Cera Gaviria stated that his government was going to hold peace talks with the drug dealers and their terrorist friends.

The so-called "peace initiatives" are nothing but a complete capitulation to the Colombian drug lord's demands. There would be no more talk of extradition to the United States. That much emerged from a five-day visit to Washington by Gaviria, during which the Bush administration gave its seal of approval of the sell-out to the cocaine barons. Bush called the plan "courageous and heroic." The years spent in gathering real hard evidence against the drug lords is now valueless; it has been compromised in such a manner that it can never be used in court.

Bobby Seale, among others, died in vain. With the approval of the Bush administration, the M19 guerillas (FARC and the ELN terrorists and their cocaine bosses were in complete control of 33 delegates who were working to thrash out a new constitution for Colombia. All in all, some

77 delegates have been charged with this responsibility.

The cocaine barons were laughing openly at the DEA and U.S. Customs Service, and no wonder. They will now have a field day in Colombia with little to fear from their impotent government, and less still from Washington. According to a copy of the *El Spectator* newspaper of February 18, 1992, which I received and translated from Spanish, this paper appears to be the only one with enough courage to speak out against the Gaviria-Bush sell out:

> Under pressure from blackmail and crime, the state refrains from exercising its fundamental responsibility to protect human life and instead agrees to negotiate away, one by one, the juridical principles that underlie the very existence of the state.

The Bush claim of victory in the non-existent "drug war" is deceitful. If it weren't such a serious matter, the administrations' statistics would be a bad joke. In February 2004, the Bush administration released the report of the National Drug Control Strategy, prepared by the new drug boss in the White House, ex- Governor Bob Martinez of Florida. Martinez got the job after William Bennett lost his war with Attorney General Thornburgh. This is just another of the thousands of cases of jobs for pals.

Former Governor John Ellis Bush (Jeb Bush), the son of G.W.H. Bush and brother of George W. Bush, was on former Governor Martinez's staff as commerce secretary. Jeb Bush was actually in deep trouble, which never surfaced. His name in selling cocaine to the Nicaraguan government was in the report that Lt. Colonel North did not believe - and successfully smothered. The badly flawed Bush document is filled with cooked statistics. DEA agents privately called it "utter trash."

When John Lawn was still head of the DEA he and his agents used to have a lot of fun with Reagan's statement that the war on drugs "has turned the corner." John Lawn is gone, but the memory of the debacle lingers on. The Bush administration pointed with pride to the $65 million emergency aid package for Colombia's "war on drugs."

Major General Miguel Gomez Padilla of Colombia's National Police Force stated that all the wrong equipment was sent and that the aid package was fine for conventional warfare, but totally useless "in the kind of warfare we are fighting."

Can America be that stupid? I don't think so. It is more likely that what happened with the Colombian aid package was a deliberately planned act of sabotage.

After twenty years of experience in the Colombian drug war, one would imagine that our government would have accumulated enough understanding to know what kind of equipment is needed. The Drug Control Strategy Reports did not give any information on the availability of drugs, nor the number of confirmed users. Nor did it deal with the most crucial issue of all; going after the user, which DEA deep cover agents have long advocated as the most likely tactic to succeed.

No wonder the U.S. government is saying very little about the huge increase in drug consumption! With marijuana now the top cash crop in 37 states, how is this "trade" going to be stopped? It will be interesting to see what happens when high grade potent seedless marijuana called "sinsemellia" starts to be cultivated in the U.S.

As long as the price of cocaine exceeds the price of gold, ($5000 per kilo) and as long as the price of heroin is six times that of an equivalent weight in gold, there will be no stamping out the drug trade, at least not with corruption at the top spreading all the way through the ranks of drug enforcement agencies.

The DEA is run through with strife. Formed in 1973 by President Nixon to avoid interagency strife between the Bureau of Narcotics and Dangerous Drugs and the Bureau of Customs, there is more jealousy and strife between the Customs and the DEA today, than ever before. Morale is non-existent. Where do we go from here? Not that any further shuffling around will make any difference. As long as the problem is not confronted from the top down, all efforts to curb the inflow of drugs to the United States will falter and fail. For real war, the top people in the highest offices in the land have to be hit, and hit hard. I have no idea who is going to be brave enough to take on the task, but we surely need a fearless leader.

The administration has lost control; it does not know the extent of the drug problem in the land. The Drug Abuse Warning Network reports that drug overdoses are not down, as contended by the Bush administration; rather they have largely gone unreported because hospital budgets have been so badly slashed that there is no money to hire the necessary staff to monitor overdose cases.

And what about Panama, since the kidnapping of General Noriega made the territory safe for the drug trade? I recall that back in 1982 I reported that Banco Nacional de Panama increased its cash flow of dollars by nearly 500 percent, this according to statistics provided by the U.S. Treasury Department. Some $6 billion in unreported money went from the U.S. to Panama in that year alone. My sources say that since the kidnapping of General Noriega, Banco Nacional de Panama has reached an all-time high in cash flow. This should have troubled the Bush administration, but there have been few, if any, signs of concern from the White House.

The banking structure in Panama was set up by Nicolas Ardito Barletta. Barletta was acceptable because he formerly ran the Marine and Midland Bank, which was taken over by the drug banker's bank, the Hong Kong and Shanghai Bank. Barletta has all the necessary experience in handling very large amounts of dope cash. When Noriega upset Barletta that is when the Bush administration made its move to get rid of the general.

In the false name of "Free Trade," we have witnessed an alarming increase in the volume of drugs available in the U.S. Cocaine has never been as cheap as it is now, and nor has it ever been so readily available. One of the most important promoters of "free trade" is the Mont Pelerin Society. It is a great pity that so many rightwing patriots are still being taken in by this organization.

I do not profess to know what the answers to the terrible menace of the drug trade are. One thing I do know is that something urgent and something drastic will have to be done, because even as I write this book, there are powerful forces at work who are trying to persuade the American people that the solution to the drug problem is to legalize drugs. I do not believe that for one minute. Legalizing the use of drugs will turn America into a nation of drug addicts in the manner in which the British East India Company turned the Chinese into a nation of opium addicts. Perhaps that is the whole idea of it; after all, it is the descendants of the British East India Company and their blue- blood Yankee partners who are running the show. As for the "drug war," it never got off the ground. It was always, and will always remain a phony drug war.

Panama under Siege is the most important expose of the drug trade from the top down I have ever written. Yet sadly, it has not received the attention it merits, probably because the title tells little about the contents. If you need to be convinced that the Bush Drug War was a phony war, then read the following chapter. You will discover that the war on drugs in Panama is non-existent, even as it is here in the United States. The U.S. State Department has its own narcotics intelligence service.

Periodically it will issue glowing reports on how it is doing in the "war on drugs." The State Department's report on Panama is typical of the hypocrisy displayed by the Bush administration. In its report, the State Department advises which nations have been "certified" as drug fighters, and these nations then get funds from the U.S. government for this purpose. Just recently Panama was "certified" as a drug-fighting nation, and thus entitled to a handout from the U.S. Can you believe it! The truth is that since the forced removal of General Noriega, Panama is the safe haven for drug dealers and their money laundering banks. Yet the State Department blurb says that

> "in the years after the military action that removed General Noriega, Panama joined the international effort to fight drugs."

The Endara government has taken important steps against money laundering, made record drug seizures and entered into important narcotics control agreements with the U.S. government.

This is utter, unadulterated, arrant nonsense. This badly flawed report proves just that the Bush Drug War is of no worth, and it becomes even more clearly phony when we consider that for years, nothing was done to stop Syrian drug trafficking and heroin refining in the Bekka Valley of Lebanon, until a few years ago, when acting on complaints from Israel - not related to the drug trade but to security issues - Syrian troops moved out of the Bekka Valley.

Chapter Four

Panama Under Siege

I n order for us to arrive at a clear understanding of what is happening in Panama — an area vital to the national security and commercial interests of the United States of America - we must go back to the drug trade centered in Hong Kong. Ever since the British established Hong Kong as a trans-shipment gold-trading point for heroin, the city has assumed an importance which belies its more generally known television and textiles image.

If Hong Kong were only a normal trading center, there would be no booming gold market there. But the old aristocratic oligarchist families of England made their massive fortunes out of shipping opium from Bengal to China. And payment was always in gold.

The British and their intertwined, interlocked old American Eastern Liberal Establishment families and their network of venerable law firms on Wall Street, banks, family brokerage and investment houses, have done the same thing to the United States that they did to China, and to a lesser extent, the Western world. As the American cocaine "trade" began to outstrip trade in heroin, so Panama grew to become the leading sheltered banking area in the world, a safe haven for the huge waves of cash flooding in.

The Hollywood crowd made cocaine a "recreational drug" and popularized its use just as they had glamorized bootleg whiskey during the "Roaring Twenties" in fictionalized accounts of how fashionable it was to drink Bronfman's brew which poured into the U.S. from Canada. The booze barons of yesteryear became the dope barons of today. Nothing much has changed except that the mechanics of distribution and concealment have become a great deal more sophisticated. No more Thompson sub-machine guns, no more loud mobsters in regalia that would make us blush. That has all gone — today it is the gentlemanly image of the boardroom and the exclusive clubs of London, New York, Hong Kong, Las Vegas and the watering holes of Nice, Monte Carlo and Acapulco. The oligarchy still maintains a discreet distance from their court servants; untouchable, serene in their palaces and their power.

The protocol is still there as are the murders. We still find the cocaine mafia routinely "executing," i.e. murdering in their unmistakable manner, those they believe to have double-crossed them. The victim is stripped of underwear, hands tied, blindfolded and shot once in the left side of the head. This is the "trade mark" of the cocaine killers; a warning to others not to try and take off with their money or dope, or start up in business on their own. The clever ones who manage to escape the assassin's bullet are simply denounced to the authorities.

Most of what passes for "drug busts" comes from information given by the top dope merchants to put the new boys, the independents, out of business. High-level protection doesn't always work when the "bosses" are robbed, as the 25-year old son of General Ruben Dario Paredes, former head of Panama's National Guard and vociferous enemy of General Manuel Noriega, found out;

he ended up in a grave in Colombia "dressed" by the cocaine killers, with a bullet hole in his left temple.

Not even his father's position could protect him from the wrath of the cocaine cartel bosses. With the Chinese Government pressing hard for a bigger slice of the opium/heroin pie, and demanding greater control of the lucrative Hong Kong gold and opium trade, top-level British controllers began to promote Panama as an "alternative" for their banking operations. Not that Panama will ever replace Hong Kong; in reality Hong Kong controls the opium/heroin trade, while Panama controls the cocaine trade - but the two overlap to a considerable degree.

Readers should understand what I am talking about here. I am not talking about companies that don't live up to expectations, I am not talking about companies that sometimes make considerable losses like "safe" nice General Motors for instance, that do not always come up to snuff. No, I am talking about a giant entity that always makes huge profits, year after year after year and never disappoints its "investors."

In 2007 the offshore dope trade exceeded $500 billion per annum and is growing annually. In 2005 the figure was estimated at $200 billion by the DEA, not a bad "growth" rate on a relatively small "investment." This huge amount of cash remains outside the laws of all countries as it crosses international boundaries with impunity. Is the drug business conducted in the "bootlegging" manner? Do sinister-looking men travel around with suitcases stuffed with $100 dollar bills?

They do on rare occasions, but mainly the dope business

can only be transacted with the witting and willing co-operation of international banks and their allied financial institutions. It is really as simple as that. Close down the drug banks, and the drug trade will begin to dry up as law enforcement agencies pounce on the drug barons pushed into the open through being forced to use desperate, and for them, dangerous alternative methods. In other words, close up the rat holes and it will be easier to get rid of the rodents. While it is gratifying to note as we do from time to time have drug arrests made and large amounts of dope seized by the authorities, this is only a drop in the ocean compared with the total volume. They come about as the result of informing on "unregistered" competitors. Such "busts" represent far less than the proverbial tip of the iceberg. And with their private intelligence systems, often far more sophisticated than those of most smaller countries, the big drug barons and their bankers usually stay several steps ahead of law enforcement agencies.

The path to successfully combating the drug menace, which is a greater danger to civilization than was the Black Death of the Middle Ages, lies through the marbled lobbies and beautifully decorated banking halls of the world. We are approaching the problem from the most difficult angle. We are trying to catch the operators, instead of going after the financiers. British banks have been in control of offshore drug banking for centuries, as indeed they have been in charge of the diamond and gold trades, both intimately connected with the heroin trade.

That is why Queen Victoria sent the most powerful army in the world at that time (1899) to crush the two tiny Boer Republics in South Africa; simply to gain control of their gold and diamonds, which Lord Palmerston, Sir Alfred Milner and Joseph Chamberlain saw as an excellent way to finance their business without the possibility of tracing payments back to the source. This is still the medium by which the Hong Kong heroin trade is largely financed. After all, gold and diamonds are impersonal.

It explains why Queen Elizabeth was more often than not at loggerheads with Mrs. Thatcher over policy matters. The Queen wanted an end to the South African Government and its antidrug stands. The Queen wanted to send a Mr. Furhop in there to run things the way he runs affairs for her in Rhodesia (now Zimbabwe). Furhop is the real name of her court messenger, better known as "Tiny" Rowland, who heads the giant conglomerate LONRHO of which she is the principle stockholder through Angus Ogilvie, her first cousin. In a sense, South Africa and Panama were both under siege for the same reasons.

The South Africans were standing in the way of a take-over of their treasure trove of gold and diamonds by the oligarchist- aristocracy and in the case of Panama, their treasured bank secrecy was being torn apart by General Noriega. The powers that be are hardly likely to take these reverses lying down! To give some idea of what is at stake in Panama, the DEA estimates that close to $350 million per day changes hands through teletype bank transfers. This is called "Interbank Money Some fifty percent of Interbank money is derived from the dope trade goes to the Cayman Islands, the Bahamas, Andorra, Panama, Hong Kong and the Swiss banks who handle this vast flow of money. As a spin-off of the dope trade, we have to contend with the burden of "floating currency exchange rates."

This destabilizing effect was brought on by the huge volume of cash, which our system was not designed to handle; there is no way that fixed rates of exchange could handle the vast and rapid transfer of money under fixed parities around the world in one day. The "economists" sold us a false bill of goods when they approved the policy of "floating" exchange rates, and they invented all sorts of economic jargon to cover the real reason viz - the huge flow of dope cash!

With a very large part of this money flowing into Panama, it was necessary to have an asset in Panama who could be trusted to maintain bank secrecy of the tightest order. The DEA estimates that $3 billion per annum disappears from the U.S. alone and finds its way to Panama. Coudert Brothers, the "mob lawyers" for the Eastern Liberal Establishment set to work in the person of Sol Linowitz, a trusted messenger for the "Olympians." He created General Omar Torrijos and packaged and sold him to the American people as a "Panamanian nationalist." His "made by David Rockefeller" stamp was carefully concealed from the vast majority of the American people.

Thanks to the treachery of sold-out servants of the CFR in the Senate, men like Dennis De Concini and Richard Lugar, Panama passed into the hands of General Torrijos at the cost of millions of dollars to the U.S. taxpayer. But Torrijos, like so many of us mortals, quickly forgot who his "maker" was, and the gods of Olympus were forced to remove him from the scene. Torrijos was duly assassinated in August 1981. Ostensibly he was killed in a plane crash, which closely resembles the type of "accident," which overtook the son of Aristotle Onassis.

What happened was that an unknown person or persons altered the mechanics of the wing flaps, so that when lowered for a landing, they actually made the plane fly upwards. Torrijos was originally handpicked by Kissinger in the manner to which we are now accustomed. When he began taking his role as a Panamanian "nationalist" seriously instead of ventriloquist's dummy, he had to go. Kissinger got himself appointed to head the President's Bipartisan Committee on Central America; another of Reagan's broken promises. This strengthened his hold on Panama, or so he thought.

We have to look at Panama through the eyes of the Trojan horse, that is to say, we must look at Central America as Kissinger's Andes plan saw it, a killing ground for thousands of American soldiers. Kissinger's orders were to get another "Vietnam War" going in the region. Panama was central to the plan. But Torrijos had other ideas. He wanted to join the Contadora Group seeking to bring stability and solutions to poverty in the region through real industrial progress. Now I am not committed to the Contadoras; there are many areas where I differ from them. But one cannot deny that the Contadoras by and large are committed to fight the drug economy planned for Central America along the lines of Jamaica's Ganja economy.

This so-called "free trade" idea is supported by members of the Mont Pelerin Society, notably Cisneros of Venezuela and the Venetian Cini Foundation. For this reason and for threatening to expose the Rockefeller banking set-up in Panama, Torrijos was "permanently immobilized," intelligence parlance for murdered.

As I have said before, we are not talking about small-time dealers or street pushers, which Hollywood delights to portray as the drug trade. We are talking major banks and financial institutions; we are talking top people; we are talking about nations that support and shelter the drug barons, countries like Cuba; and we are talking about an organization so strong and powerful that it has brought an entire country to its knees, the Republic of Colombia.

I am going to be writing about U.S. State Department complicity in hindering the war on drugs. I am going to talk about Nancy Reagan's unbelievably stupid response "Just Say No" to this menace. When compared with what is transpiring today, the volume of heroin flowing through the "French Connection" was strictly penny ante stuff. Yet, we must never lose sight of the fact that ex-President Richard Nixon was the only President to firmly tackle the drug menace threatening the U.S. The "French Connection" was a Nixon endeavor from start to finish. For his insolence in taking on the drug trade from the top down, he was removed from office, disgraced, ridiculed and humiliated by the Watergate scam as a lesson and a warning to others who might wish to follow his example. By comparison, President Reagan's "war on drugs" was merely an answer blowing in the wind! The "Circle of Initiates," who founded the Royal Institute for International Affairs has not changed its direction. It is worth repeating that the drug trade is firmly controlled by the descendants and families who intermarried, and who comprise this inner secret society membership, who can trace their lineage to Lords Alfred Milner, Gray, Balfour, Palmerston, Rothschild and others at the top of Debrett's Peerage and America's Social Register.

Their banks and the American banks are no small fry. In fact the smaller banks have been weeded out or are in the process of being weeded out with witting or perhaps unwitting help of the U.S. Treasury Department. This is particularly evident in Florida, where starting in 1977 big banks like the Standard and Chartered Bank, Bank Hapolum, well-known as banks involved in laundering dirty dope money, moved into Florida where the "action" was. The "big boys" then began informing on small banks used by small independent cocaine dealers. Remember, the drug monopolists have their own highly efficient intelligence network. The Treasury went after the small banks, but left the big ones alone. When big banks are caught, which has happened on a few occasions, they are dealt with in a most lenient fashion.

Witness the case of Credit Suisse in Geneva and First Bank of Boston. This most venerable of Boston's banks was caught red handed laundering dope money in conjunction with Credit Suisse. Some 1200 separate indictments were brought against the First National. The Justice Department combined the charges into a single charge, and the bank was given a light slap on the wrist with a measly $500 fine! Credit Suisse was not pursued by the Justice Department or the Treasury! Credit Suisse remains one of the largest and most efficient dope money laundering banks after American Express — the "untouchables" of the banking world.

Other major banks involved in the lucrative dirty-money business of dope were National Westminster, Barclays, Midlands Bank and the Royal Bank of Canada. The Royal Bank of Canada and the National Westminster Bank were the key drug bankers for the dope barons in the Caribbean Islands David Rockefeller's much vaunted "Caribbean Basin Initiative." Working through the IMF, Kissinger ordered Jamaica to grow a "free enterprise" crop of ganja (marijuana) which today accounts for the bulk of Jamaica's foreign exchange earnings. The same thing happened in Guyana, which is why Jim Jones moved there — except that Jones was unaware of the true purpose of his manipulators. As part of a massive brainwashing experiment of the Vacaville type, Jones never did reach his goal. He died in total ignorance of those who were pulling his strings.

Jamaica is just one of the countries run on dope money. When he was in charge of Jamaica, Edward Seaga quite brazenly told American newspapers, notably the Washington Post, that whether it is accepted or not "the industry, as such, is here to stay. It is just not possible to wipe it out." I have no quarrel with the "here to stay" bit. Using rock and roll "music" as its vehicle for the spread of "recreational drugs" and protected at the highest levels, the drug trade indeed seems destined to stay on.

That is not to say that it cannot be eliminated. The first steps in an eradication program would, in my opinion, be to attack its major banks and to pass legislation making the sale of rock and roll music in all its forms — cassettes, discs etc. and promoting rock concerts — a criminal offence punishable by stiff prison sentences.

As one of the spin-offs of the "meat-grinder war" between Iran and Iraq, the sale of heroin from which diacecyl morphine is derived skyrocketed. Most of the proceeds of this trade found its way into Panamanian banks, the "overlap" with Hong Kong, which I mentioned earlier.

There are officially 2.6 million heroin addicts in Iran of which 1.5 million are in the army, where soldiers-addicts can get it on request. One recalls, that the British oligarchy tried the same deal during the War Between the States, the Civil War, but did not have any success. Not only has heroin money fueled the Gulf War, it also fuels "freedom fighters" outfits, a term used by George Shultz to describe the murderous African National Congress (ANC), Basque Separatists (ETA), the Irish Republic Army (IRA), the Sikh separatist movement, the Kurds et al. The funds, derived from the sale of opium and cocaine, are channeled to these terrorist organizations through the World Council of Churches.

From the foregoing it becomes clear why Panama is so important to the supra-national One World forces. Panama's banking system was set up by David Rockefeller to be a convenient banking depository for dope trade money. Panama was adjudicated the banking center for cocaine, while Hong Kong remained the heroin-opium center. Panama's banking system was restructured according to Rockefeller's blueprint by Nicholas Ardito Barletta, a former director of the World Bank, and a director of the Marine Midland Bank, which was taken over by the king of drug banks, the Hong Kong and Shanghai Bank, Barletta was acceptable because of his "respectable" image and experience in handling vast amounts of dope cash. In 1982, the Treasury Department estimated that the Banco Nacional de Panama had increased its cash flow of dollars by nearly 500 percent between 1980 and 1984. Some $6 billion in unreported money went from the U.S. to Panama during this four-year period alone.

Former President Alan Garcia of Peru, who led an all-out war against the dope barons, addressed the United Nations on September 23, 1998, on this subject and listed Peru's successes and victories in the war on drugs. He went to say:

> We could therefore ask the American administration if we have done that in fifty days, what it is doing for the human rights of the individual keeling over in Grand Central Station and so many other places, and when will it legally and in a Christian fashion, fight to eradicate the consumption?

Mrs. Nancy Reagan's response was, "Just Say No," but that is no answer to President Garcia's implicit charge that the U.S. is doing well below its best to eradicate the drug curse. Yet so many so-called "economists" still call for legalizing this vile business in the name of "free trade."

Among them we find Diego Cisneros who is a member of the Mont Pelerin Society, a so-called Conservative body that promotes the theory of "free trade." After the assassination of Omar Torrijos in August 1961 (he was assassinated because he chose to ignore Henry Kissinger's orders and was showing strong signs of going it alone), strong man General Rueben Paredes took control of Panama. But in February 1981, he went down the wrong road, threatening to expel the American ambassador from Panama for interfering in the country's internal affairs. Kissinger thereupon delivered a message to Paredes.

In an amazing "about-face," General Paredes suddenly began supporting Kissinger's Andean Plan to turn Central America into another Vietnam for the U.S. military, abandoning support for Contadora policies. Although it has many flaws, basically the Contadora Group was aware of the Kissinger "Trojan horse" in Central America, and it tried hard to prevent a Vietnam-style conflict from developing in the region. Henry Kissinger and the U.S. State Department had previously promoted Paredes as a "Panama nationalist, a staunch anti-Communist friend of America."

On a Kissinger sponsored visit to Washington D.C. Paredes was escorted around by Kissinger in person. Six months after the murder of Torrijos, General Paredes took command of the National Guard. Thereafter, Paredes openly praised The FARC terrorists of Colombia, and sabotaged Contadora's efforts to arrive at a peaceful solution to the problems of the region. He also took great pains to cultivate the friendship of Anulfo Arias, whom the Washington Post, the New York Times and surprisingly, Senator Jesse Helms, held up as the rightful heir to the leadership of Panama, whose position was allegedly usurped by General Noriega. Strangely enough, during the Panama Canal Treaty hearings, the media jackals said nothing about Torrijos usurping Anulfo Arias's "rightful" position! A lot of nonsense has been talked about Arias being a "Nazi" and therefore unworthy to lead Panama. This kind of anti-German propaganda is not worthy of comment.

Notwithstanding the merciless cocaine mafia-style execution of his 25 year old son along with two other Panamanian "business partners" by killers who work for the Ochoa and Escobar clans, Paredes has remained loyal to the drug overlords and their banking nexus. The loss of Panamanian support was a big blow to the aspirations of the Contadoras. It meant that Panama would remain a "wide open" center for financing sales of weapons to the region, notably supplied by Israel under an agreement reached between local leaders and the late Ariel Sharon, a former business partner of Kissinger.

Apart from threats for which Kissinger is notorious, the IMF had a hand in blackmailing Paredes. My sources told me that Kissinger let it be known, that the IMF stand-by agreement to restructure Panama's $320 million debt might not hold good if Paredes fell out with his master. Paredes "got the message." The IMF immediately began a struggle with General Noriega who told the Panamanian people in a televised address on March 22, 1986, that the IMF is strangling Panama.

President Eric Delville unfortunately backed IMF austerity packages, which were designed to weaken labor union support for Noriega. The CONATO labor federation then began threatening to break with General Noriega, unless the IMF dictates were ignored.

General Manuel Noriega, while still Colonel Noriega, was chief of the anti-narcotics bureau in Panama and battled for ten years to keep the Panama National Guard free of the taint of corruption that follows in the wake of dope money, as surely as day follows night. With the Ochoa and Escobar families virtually taking over Panama, this was no mean feat. Noriega's anti-drug struggle was confirmed by John C. Lawn, head of the Drug Enforcement Agency (DEA). Lawn was not known for flowery speeches nor writing letters of commendation. His letter to General Noriega was therefore all the more remarkable, in that it lavished praise on him in an unstinting manner.

Here is an excerpt from that letter, which is representative of the manner, and style in which it is couched:

> *I would like to take this opportunity to reiterate my deep appreciation for the vigorous anti-drug trafficking policy that you have adopted, which is reflected in the numerous expulsions from Panama of accused traffickers, the large seizures of cocaine and precursor chemicals that have occurred in Panama and the eradication of marijuana cultivation in Panama territory.*

Neither the *Washington Post* nor the *New York Times* saw fit to reprint this commendation, which appeared in a newspaper in Peru. I will go back to the subject of the DEA and John C. Lawn later, because of its vital significance.

The only thing the *Washington Post* did to counter this fine testimonial was to publish untruths by its so-called "intelligence expert," Seymour Hersh, who wrote an article in which he stated that General Noriega was a "double agent" for the CIA, feeding it with information he received from Cuba. This is a ploy well- known to genuine intelligence people. The purpose of such "disclosures" would be to get Cuban DGI secret service assassins to murder General Noriega on the pretext, that he "double-crossed Cuba." This would draw attention away from the Kissinger-bankers gang if the assassination attempt were to prove successful. Hersh's information and stories have often not been very accurate and the Noriega "disclosure" should be seen for what it was; a possible set-up for an assassination attempt on General Noriega.

Noriega fought back with all of the meager resources at his disposal. But let it be known that any move against the drug trade is fraught with peril.

Panama was an example of the kind of counteraction a powerful enemy is capable of mounting. In the Caribbean and Panama, anti-drug forces were faced with a consortium made up of Coudert Brothers law firm in the person of Sol Linowitz. Among other members of the consortium were Fidel Castro, David Rockefeller, Henry Kissinger and the International Monetary Fund (IMF), plus a number of top banks and the U.S. State Department. Kissinger's Andes Plan was being stymied by General Noriega and he came under fire because of his antidrug stance. The outcome in Panama could be foretold. Rockefeller's Caribbean Basin Initiative amounted to handing Fidel Castro a dope empire worth at least $35 billion per annum, which had no intention of giving it up without a struggle.

In Colombia, David Rockefeller and Kissinger created "a state within a state," where Carlos Lederer — until his arrest — was a kingpin in the Ochoa and Escobar clans who virtually ruled the whole country. In downtown Bogota, half the city's magistrates were executed by the drug barons' private MI9 Guerilla army also known as (FARC).

The assault was an outright act of anarchy that left Colombia in a state of numbed fear. What was behind all the frantic activity, which in reality was a revolution? Quite simply — it was cash, wave and wave of cash, flowing into the offshore havens of the Caribbean and Panama. The DEA estimates that Colombia alone banked $39 billion in cash from 1980-2006. The DEA and the Treasury believed that Panama had become the banking capital of the cocaine world, and I have no quarrel with its assessment. In 1982 the Treasury Department stated that Banco National de Panama had become the main clearinghouse for drug dollars with a six-fold increase in its cash flow from 1980 to 1988.

Panama, up until the advent of General Noriega taking power, was also the favored meeting place for kingpins of the drug trade. Lopez Michelson, who offered to pay off Colombia's external debt from cocaine revenues if the Colombian Government would "legalize" the position of the dope families, operated quite freely out of Panama, where he often met Jorge Ochoa and Pablo Escobar. These top members of the Colombia dope cartel were known to have struck a deal with Rodrigo Botera Montoya, Colombia's finance minister from 1974-1976 who set up an "open window" at the Central Bank, where dope dollars could be freely and openly traded without any hassle from the authorities. That "window" has never been closed! It is better known by its colloquial name "ventanilla siniestra" literally "sinister window." It was through this "window" that Fidel Castro received huge amounts of U.S. dollars.

Were U.S. authorities aware of Botera's activites? Of course they were. Botera was a member of the prestigious Aspen Institute, the Ford Foundation and a former co-chairman of the Inter American Dialogue. He was well known to the suave Elliott Richardson, whom we will best remember for his persecution and betrayal of President Richard Nixon in the aftermath of the Watergate scandal. Not so well known is the fact that Elliott Richardson, an upper crust eminently respectable Boston Brahmin, was the late Cyrus Hashemi's lawyer. Hashemi was the number one gunrunner for the 1979 Carter-Khomeini arms deal.

Richardson was the registered representative and legal advisor for the Marxist Government of Angola. He was also heavily involved in the scandalous cover-up of the mysterious deaths of 9 mental patients at the sinister Bridgeport facility, which up to the present day still has not been investigated. Richardson's ties to the dope trade are visible through the pro-narcotics lobby, the Institute for Liberty and Democracy, which he helped to found in Lima, Peru in 1961.

With so many names cropping up in the unfolding Panama tragedy, it seems advisable to list the principal players and institutions involved - especially Noriega's enemies who were numerous and powerful as the following list shows:

Alvin Weeden Gamboa

A Panamanian lawyer and courier for the drug barons formed the Popular Action Party (PAPO), an opposition party to champion human rights, together with two other Noriega enemies, Winston Robles and Roberto Eisenmann. All were strongly opposed to the Panama Defense Force and regularly received lavish praise from the U.S. jackal press and the State Department, who classed them as members of an "alternative democratic government" of Panama.

Cesar Tribaldos

He was heavily implicated in money laundering for the Colombian cocaine barons. He is and was a coordinator of the Civic Crusade movement along with Roberto Eisenmann, owner of the La Prensa newspaper and member of PAPO. He was also on the board of Banco Continental.

Ricardo Tribaldos

The brother of Cesar, he was indicted for trying to import into Panama, huge quantities of the precursor chemical ethyl ether (Acetone), the principal chemical used to refine cocaine. Ricardo had set up the operation in 1984 in anticipation of Colombians Ochoa and Escobar opening a major cocaine laboratory-processing operation in Panama.

Roberto Eisenmann

Roberto Eisenmann was the owner of the La Prensa newspaper and at the time, a powerful asset of the U.S. State Department. He figured prominently in the proposed "alternative democratic" government for Panama. Eisenmann hated Noriega for wrecking one of Jorge Genoa's major operations and closing down First Interamerica Bank, which was violating Panama's 1985 bank laws. This left Eisenmann and his colleagues reeling.

No one had expected that any serious action could or would ever be taken against the international community controlling 80% of Panama's economy, which "interests" had founded a "Switzerland in Panama," following the changes made by Nicholas Barletta. It therefore amazed this elite community of narcotics traffickers and bankers, when Noriega provided this information to the DEA, which resulted in the arrest of major cocaine baron Jorge Ochoa in Spain. The Panama establishment was jolted by these developments.

Eisenmann became a vociferous critic of Noriega, accusing him of destroying Panama's economy, even accused him of being implicated in the cocaine trade, when in fact it was Eisenmann who worked closely with the Colombian cocaine barons. Eisenmann was one of a gaggle of drug barons, bankers, lawyers and newspaper editors, whose pro-democracy rhetoric was designed to cover their tracks, which, had the truth been unveiled, would have led their tracks straight to cocaine dirty money laundering. Eisenmann, who led the attack on Noriega for 12 years, was the first choice of the U.S. State Department to head up the government it intended placing in power once Noriega was ousted. There may be readers who will view this information with skepticism, but I am confident that my information will stand any test as it is backed by solid facts. In 1964, Eisenmann was exposed as the man behind the purchase of Dadeland Bank of Miami, through which the Fernandez syndicate laundered its cocaine and marijuana, enough proof, that banks could justifiably have been investigated by the DEA. But that did not happen.

The Fernandez syndicate, indicted in 1984, stored large

amounts of cash benefits from the dope trade in rented safe deposit boxes at the bank prior to transferring it to Panama, and court records show that the syndicate held a majority of the total issued stock in Eisenmann's Dadeland Bank. Yet it was Weeden, Eisenmann and Fernandez, who specifically charged Noriega with dealing with the dope barons. After the publicity, the Fernandez syndicate transferred its dirty money from Dadeland Bank to Banco de Iberoamerica, named in the indictment as one of 15 Panamanian banks it used. Eisenmann later swore that he had no idea that his Dadeland Bank was being used for laundering narcotics money.

Carlos Rodriguez Milian

This remarkable courier for Lederer, Escobar and the Ochoa brothers, was paid a salary of $2 million per month up until the time of his arrest by DEA agents following a tip they received from his sworn enemy, General Noriega. His job involved supervision and delivery of huge sums of drug cash to Bank of America, First Boston and Citicorp, among others, for laundering.

At the Senate Foreign Relations Subcommittee on Narcotics hearing on February 11, 1988, proceedings that were designed to smear and blacken the name of General Noriega. Milian was brought from prison, where he is serving a 43-year sentence for drug related business activities, to testify against General Noriega. But he disrupted proceedings and scared Committee members by disclosing that he had delivered huge loads of drug dollars to several American banks, His unexpected unsolicited disclosures under oath were totally blacked out by the jackals of the U.S. news media.

Lt. Colonel Julian Melo Borbua

Dishonorably discharged from the Panama National Guard in 1964, Borbua became one of the star witnesses against Noriega. While still in the National Guard, he met with the Ochoa brothers in Colombia, who gave him the job and paid him 5 million to open a cocaine laboratory at Darien, in the Panama jungle; to secure safe storage and transit facilities and safe- housing for weapons for sale, mainly of Israeli origin, and to set- up arrangements with various banks to facilitate the flow of cash from these illegal transactions. Compatriots in the scheme were Ricardo Tribaldos, the man who was indicted for trying to import ethyl ether into Panama, and one Gabriel Mendez.

Tribaldos and Mendez knew they were up against it when Noriega's men began destroying large shipments of ethyl ether acid and located and wrecked a large cocaine laboratory. Under the direction of undisclosed persons, Tribaldos, Mendez and Borbua planned massive flight capital from Panama.

The plan called for an attack and smear campaign against the military, and if possible, to have Noriega assassinated. But before any of it could be carried out, the Panama Defense Force (PDF) discovered the plot and arrested the trio. Mendez and Tribaldos were charged with narcotics trafficking and went to prison, but were released by a Panama court under suspicious circumstances. Borbua was dishonorably discharged from the PDF. They all became active members of the Civic Crusade front, set-up to oust General Noriega.

Civic Crusade

This front for Eisenmann and his associates was solely a vehicle for use against General Noriega. Its backers were Eisenmann, Barletta, Tribaldos, Castillo and Blandon, Elliott Richardson, Norman Bailey and Sol Linowitz. The Civic Crusade established itself in Washington D.C. in June 1987, and Lewis Galindo, the self-described "international representative of Panama's opposition to Noriega" was employed to run it.

Galindo has impeccable credentials with the Shultz faction of the State Department and the Eastern Liberal Establishment through the Trilateral Commission and Sol Linowitz, one of the Olympian's most trusted servants and a partner in the prestigious law firm of Coudert Brothers. It was the same law firm, that was to betray the U.S. by giving away U.S. sovereign territory at Panama, which very importantly is forbidden by the U.S. Constitution; Galindo also had impeccable credentials with the former President of Colombia, Alfonso Lopez Michelson, generally regarded by narcotics intelligence agents as the man who acted as overseer of the Colombian cocaine and marijuana trade during his term in office from 1974 to 1978.

The Robles Brothers

Ivan Robles and his brother Winston are prominent lawyers in Panama. They owe their prominence to the cocaine trade bosses and their bankers. Winston Robles is a co-editor of Roberto Eisenmann's La Prensa with its proven Fernandez-Dadeland Bank connections. The International Law Directory gives the correct title of the law firm as Martindale-Hubbell, Robles and Robles. Eisenmann of La

Prensa, also a proven one-third owner of the Dadeland Bank, with its unsavory past connections to the Fernandez syndicate, was favored by former Secretary of State George Shultz and the State Department to replace General Noriega.

These "negotiations" stemmed from the totally false drug trafficking charges brought against Noriega by a Miami Florida grand jury on February 5, 1988. This indictment again points up the most urgent need for the American people to rid themselves of this archaic, feudal "star chamber" (Grand Jury) appendage to our legal system. The latest information on the "negotiations" is George Shultz's statement:

> We have had a lot of discussion with him (Noriega), but we have not yet concluded any agreement that the charges against Noriega will be dropped if he voluntarily steps down.

Admiral John Poindexter

The false charges against Noriega arose out of the failed mission of Poindexter to force the General to relinquish his post. Poindexter's mission on behalf of Shultz was along the lines of President Reagan's blunt message to get rid of President Marcos, delivered through Senator Paul Laxalt, who played the Judas role far better that did Poindexter. Poindexter's mission set in motion the current war by the drug barons, bankers, lawyers and their U.S. allies to rid Panama of the threat to their existence emanating from the vigorous prosecution of anti-cocaine banking laws and policies pursued by General Noriega and the PDF. In the Mike Wallace TV interview, Noriega made it clear that Poindexter had come as a bully demanding that Panama bow down to the colonialist demands of the Olympians (The Committee of 300).

I was not against Nicaragua being invaded by U.S. military forces; but another Vietnam-style war would only have played into the hands of One World Government and the traitors within our gates. Poindexter was backed by the U.S. media who went as far as to advocate that Noriega be removed by force. When he answered Poindexter's threats with a firm rebuff, Noriega knew that the chips were down. He thereupon sought an alliance with and support from the Peronistas. At a meeting with Peronista leaders, which took place at Mar del Plata, Argentina, Noriega and his deputation of middle-level officers received the assurances they were looking for. But it was not long before counter-measures were taken to scare the Argentineans away. British troops mounted "exercises" in the Malvinas to show what would happen if Argentina intervened in Panama's affairs, and General John Calvin, chief of the U.S. military southern area command, went to meet with Argentine Defense Minister Horacio Juanarena. Ostensibly the meeting dealt with British threats and growing tensions between the two countries over the Malvinas.

General Galvin delivered a stern warning to Juanarena for Argentina not to get involved in Panama. Galvin's mission to Buenos Aires could quite properly have been compared with General Hauser's mission to Tehran during the period that former President Jimmy Carter was betraying the Shah of Iran.

DEA drug operation coming on the heels of a three-year investigation carried out under the code name "Operations Pisces," showed that the drug barons and their supporters were the beneficiaries of enormous profits. Up to 1985 nobody had seriously troubled them. But in 1985, where before it seemed only vaguely possible that seldom used laws might become a bother to be dealt with by intimidation, bribery and corruption, Noriega was now showing that he could not be threatened or bought, and that he meant business.

"Operations Pisces" closed down 54 accounts in 18 Panamanian banks and resulted in the seizure of $10 million and large quantities of cocaine. It was later established, that the banks were warned by some in the PDF and were able to move large amounts of cash before being raided. This was followed by the freezing of another 85 accounts in banks whose deposits were believed to be stained with blood and cocaine, an action carried out by the Panama Defense Force (PDF). Fifty-eight major Colombian, U.S. and some Cuban-American "runners" were arrested and indicted on narcotics trafficking charges. "Operations Pisces" was made possible by passage of Panamanian Law 23, which gave notice of what the narcotics traffickers could expect in future. *La Prensa* complained bitterly that the Panama Defense Force was conducting a publicity campaign against drugs on behalf of the American Government, a campaign that "will devastate the Panamanian banking center."

Jose Blandon

Enter Jose Blandon, now turned 180 degrees by the pro-drug consortium. What was the role assigned to Blandon in the unfolding war against anti-cocaine forces?

He was hired to drum up so-called "international support" for Elliott Richardson-Sol Linowitz faction trying to bring down General Noriega. In so doing, Blandon exposed himself as a hypocritical unmitigated liar. Blandon served Willie Brandt's Socialist International (also known in some circles as The Partnership). Before taking up his post as chief accuser of Noriega, Blandon, who was the New York Consul General for Panama, went on Panama TV on August 11, 1987 in support of Noriega. He vehemently attacked the forces ranged against General Noriega — characterizing the hostility as a campaign essentially aimed at the liquidation of Jose Blandon.

Let us take a closer look at the State Department's "Panama" spokesman. Shortly after his television appearance in favor of Noriega, in fact in less than a month, Blandon was seized upon by the Eastern Liberal Establishment in the persons of Shultz, Kissinger and Elliot Abrams and told to stop backing the wrong horse. According to intelligence reports, Blandon was left in no uncertainty as to what the future held for Noriega. He was quite bluntly told to "join the winning team" or find himself out in the cold when the "new government" was ushered in. Blandon, who has always been a self-seeking individual, lost no time in changing course and jumping on the "get Noriega" bandwagon. Shortly after switching sides, Blandon announced that he was "gathering support from the international community against General Noriega."

He was thereupon summarily dismissed from his consular post. No government can afford to have its representatives conspiring with "foreign forces advocating its overthrow." Blandon was immediately supported by the State Department and the U.S. news media. He was touted by Dr. Norman Bailey as a respectable Panamanian official of high rank, who had really startling information to impart about Noriega's alleged "drug trafficking." I cannot be completely certain that Blandon was not immediately given financial support by Bailey, the Civic Crusade and Sol Linowitz, but Washington said he received some information that would tend to confirm Blandon was a paid hireling of Linowitz, Norman Bailey and the Civic Crusade. Miami lawyer Ray Takiff, who represented General Noriega in the U.S. said quite simply that Blandon was a liar in the pay of the U.S. Government.

One of Blandon's controllers was William G. Walker, Deputy Assistant Secretary of State for International Affairs, who later played a dirty role in bringing down the government of Serbia. According to reports I received, it was Walker who coached Blandon regarding his testimony before the mud-slinging anti-Noriega Senate Foreign Affairs Subcommittee on Terrorism, Narcotics and International Operations. Walker was later to play a key role in the destruction of Serbian leader Milosevic that brought the downfall of country with the resultant takeover by a Muslim government from Albania.

Blandon was known for his wild swings from one subject to another, not to mention changing horses in mid-stream. Walker wanted to be sure that Blandon did not stray into areas that might lead to complications, while testifying before the "open and shut" committee in the manner of Rodriguez Milian's embarrassing expose of the leading American banks. Lewis Galindo of the Civic Crusade, with whom we are now familiar, was another Blandon "coach" along with Walker and Dr. Norman Bailey. Galindo spent a lot of time telling Blandon to stick to the point, while giving his testimony to the eager "get Noriega" Senate Subcommittee.

The committee must have been familiar with Blandon's

penchant for twisting "facts" in the same way they must have known about his rather dubious "high level international contacts." Yet the Senate Subcommittee presented Blandon as its star witness against Noriega most of the time during the February 8 through 11 sessions. This should deeply disturb all patriots who value our institutions and traditions.

The attack on Noriega has degraded and debased our institutions, not to mention casting grave doubts on our justice system. Desiring to make the most of Blandon's testimony, although it would never have stood up for more than a few minutes under court rules of evidence, and under cross- examination, the committee members listened eagerly to his rambling, contradictory diatribe against General Noriega. Even with such a wide margin of latitude with committee members bending over backwards to be solicitous, Blandon cut as sorry a figure as the criminals Floyd Carlton and Milian Rodriguez, who were called as prosecution witnesses.

The proceedings were reminiscent of "show trials" and have no place in the American system. If this is what our politicians call "open government," then God help America. Could the subcommittee hearings be classified as a "trial?" I tend to believe, that it was a trial of General Noriega, although subcommittee chairman John Kerry categorically dismissed this when it was put to him. Kerry paraded Blandon before the committee as one parades a dog around the ring at a dog show. When Blandon began to babble incoherently, Kerry on numerous occasions said "stay boy — not so fast." This is the same John Kerry who was to make a run for the presidency of the United States. Thank God he was defeated.

Kerry made sure that Blandon's recent television speech in support of Noriega was not brought up. During that speech Blandon said that charges against the PDF's commander were "fabrications" and vehemently denied that any PDF officers were involved in narcotics trafficking. Now this may be good politics, but it makes for poor justice. In the end, unable to follow his own ramblings, Blandon contradicted himself and gave such widely differing accounts of the same events, that even the jackals of the media, notably *Time Magazine*, were grudgingly forced to admit that Blandon's credibility was non existent! But not with John Kerry, who could not afford to lose his Star Chamber witness.

Where did came Blandon's "facts" about Noriega's involvement in dope trafficking come from? Careful analyses prepared by specialists in this field showed a striking similarity between phrases and words used by Norman Bailey, Lopez Michelson, Roberto Eisenmann, Lewis Galindo and many of the words and expressions used by Blandon. So it appears that these men might have been putting words in Blandon's mouth. Millionaire Galindo, who is supposed to have made his fortune out of real estate, and Eisenmann of *La Prensa* we have already met, but it is useful and necessary to mention in passing, that Galindo enjoys the confidence of Trilateral Commission's Sol Linowitz and his close associate, Dr. Norman Bailey.

Lopez Michelson

Lopez Michelson was President of Colombia from 1974-1978, during which period he became very friendly with Fidel Castro who resettled Carlos Lederer after he was forced by DEA agents to flee the Bahamas. It was Michelson's finance minister, Rodrigo Bolero Montoya, who made it easy for the cocaine barons to deposit their dope dollars by opening the "sinister window" at Colombia's national bank as part of Michelson's oversight activities on behalf of cocaine barons Ochoa, Lederer and Escobar. Lopez Michelson even tried to legalize the dope barons in exchange for their offer to pay-off Colombia's external debt obligations!

Nicolas Ardito Barletta

Another of the State Department's hired lackeys was Nicolas Ardito Barletta. Friend and confidant of Norman Bailey of the National Security Council and head of the NSC-CIA "banker's branch," close to Sol Linowitz and William Colby, Barletta was obviously an important ally of the "get Noriega" faction. I have already mentioned that Panama became a haven for dope traffickers and their money laundering banks shortly after Blandon enacted strict bank secrecy laws: just in time for the cocaine trade "boom." His bank secrecy legislation was never challenged - until General Noriega took on this awesome responsibility. No wonder Blandon has allied himself with his enemies. Blandon was known in Washington as the Panama "banker's man."

Steven Sarnos

Identified as a narcotics trafficker, Sarnos appeared to enjoy surprisingly ready access to administration officials like Admiral Poindexter, and notables like Barletta. Sarnos was part of the group made up of Eisenmann, Galindo and others, who started the slander campaign against Noriega. It seems that Sarnos was another of Jose Blandon's many "coaches."

Sarnos travels to see his high-level U.S. connections under the protection of the Federal witness program. Perhaps because of evidence supplied by Sarnos, his former colleague and business partner Fernandez was hit with a prison term for marijuana dealing. We may not ever find out, but it must be the reason why Sarnos is allowed to travel to the U.S., while a man like President Waldheim, Former U.N. Secretary General, is blacklisted.

The Senate committee under John Kerry appeared to do everything in its power to offset Blandon's wildly erratic performance. When questioned by the press about Blandon's changed testimony, inaccuracies and contradictions, Senator D'Amato, one of the members, said: "Publicity people would try to do anything to discredit the testimony of Mr. Blandon." But in the end Blandon's testimony was shown to be nothing more than the product of an over-ripe imagination. His claim to have seen documents that confirmed CIA spying on the private lives of certain U.S. Senators, an allegation hotly denied by the CIA, but reconfirmed by Blandon, caused quite a stir. Blandon's CIA "bombshell" upset the committee almost as much as Milian's disclosures that top U.S. banks were involved in laundering dope cash.

Another of the "influential international figures," who supported the "get Noriega" conspiracy was Ted Turner of CNN. Turner is believed to be a member of the Trilateral Commission who was personally "turned" by David Rockefeller. It looks as though his name was added to the list of Noriega's enemies. Roberto Eisenmann's La Prensa heaved a sigh of relief at the way the Senate Subcommittee hearings went. It was apparent that the dope banker's policy for Panama would henceforth be U.S. official policy. The campaign against the PDF waged by the U.S. came straight from the pages of La Prensa with its howls of rage at being "repressed." The cocaine barons and their bankers wrote the lyrics for the song of hate being sung by the Reagan administration against the best drug trafficking fighter in the world at that period, General Manuel Noriega.

The fact, that Noriega was smeared with dirt should tell us something about just how effective he was in the war on drugs. If he were a non-entity, nobody in Washington or Panama would be bothered by him. An international hate and slander campaign came rapidly to a climax and ended in the ouster of Noriega. It is my belief based on information of the highest reliability, that even after he was forced out, Noriega remained in dire danger. That information proved to be correct with the kidnapping and transporting of Noriega to a Florida jail, followed by a kangaroo-court trial without parallel in jurisprudence of any Western nation. The dope barons and their bankers are not going to forgive and forget. Noriega was marked for elimination in the same way as General Somoza of Nicaragua was destined to be murdered.

Some good did emerge from the Subcommittee hearings. General Paul German denied that he had found any evidence of wrongdoing by Noriega as claimed by Blandon and Norman Bailey. He said there was no hard evidence that Noriega had ties to the cocaine barons. There had been rumors, said German, but no real evidence was ever found. Nor could the committee produce one shred of credible evidence to support the false charges lodged against Noriega, no matter how mightily Kerry huffed and puffed, and yet he was found guilty and sentenced to life imprisonment from which he will never be released.

Blandon, Barletta, Linowitz, Elliot Abrams, Elliott

Richardson, Lewis Galindo and Roberto Eisenmann, among others, want to see the dope trade legalized. Richardson's approach to this issue was highly ingenuous. He advocated legalizing drugs without actually appearing to do so. The line he took was that it was "too late" to attempt to fight the dope menace, and that no matter what efforts are made to suppress it, like alcohol before it, the best way to go is to legalize narcotics. This, according to Richardson and his Eastern Liberal Establishment banker's faction will prove far more effective and less costly in the long run — exactly the line adopted by Senator Edward Kennedy in his numerous attempts to legalize dope.

Edward Kennedy was spared the fate of his brothers, because he is useful for pushing establishment bills in the Senate - the sole reason for his continuing political career. If Kennedy once dares to vote against pro-narcotics legislation, he will be eliminated. We know it and he knows it. It is as unambiguous as that. In his article copied from the Sol Linowitz 1986 Report of the Inter-American Dialogue, Richardson practically quotes the arguments put forward by *La Prensa* and Carlos Lederer in support for legalizing the use of cocaine and marijuana in the same way that the U.S. was eventually forced to legalize alcohol. The Inter-American Dialogue is an Eastern Liberal Establishment-Latin American confluence of opinion, which follows Trilateral policy-making for the region, under the auspices of the Committee of 300.

In short, it is there to rubberstamp Trilateral Commission decisions. From its list of members one can quickly gauge to what extent this body was set up to carry out CFR orders. Where the names of McGeorge Bundy, Linowitz, Kissinger, John R. Petty, Robert S. McNamara, Barletta and Montoya crop up, we can rest assured that dirty work at the crossroads exists.

Courier for the Colombian cocaine barons Samper Pizano says that a new and fresh approach to the drug problem must be considered for the West. Pizano, who does not dispute his connections with the Colombian cocaine barons, once presented Lopez Michelson with a check for a very handsome amount of money as a "contribution" to his presidential campaign. The money was accepted by Michelson, even though he knew that it came from Carlos Lederer.

The hoary argument for selective legalization was also trotted out by Richardson. Apparently 65 million drug addicts in the U.S. is not a sufficient number. Richardson hints that the war against drugs cannot be won, another old and dangerous argument, which ignores the hammer-blows President Garcia was able deliver against the cocaine mafia in only fifty days, and that with strictly limited resources at his disposal! The clincher is the statement;... the illegality of drugs makes the damage greater for both addicts and societies of the Americas. As an officer of the courts, Richardson deserved to be examined by the American Bar Association, charged with pushing the sale of narcotics and indicted on such charges. The Inter-American Dialogue has its narcotics banker club backing the attempts to legalize dope. That there is a proven link between the First Bank of Boston, Credit Suisse and the cocaine barons of Colombia would not be hard to prove; much less difficult than trying to make Jose Blandon's twisted testimony credible and acceptable.

Why didn't the Senate Subcommittee, which was smearing Noriega, go after Credit Suisse, First Bank of Boston, American Express and Bank of America, if it really wanted to project credibility in battling the drug trade? What was John Kerry's role in all this? When did the State Department really begin to fear Noriega?

I would estimate that it was immediately following the success of the joint DEA-Panama anti-drug action code-named "Operations Pisces," which was publicly revealed by the DEA on May 6, 1987, in which it characterized as "the largest and most successful undercover investigation in Federal drug law enforcement history." The State Department immediately began counter-operations in conjunction with those named in this article to undercut the success of "Operation Pisces" and remove General Noriega as Commander of the Panama Defense Force. The State Department and its allies in the pro-dope lobby had good reason to fear Noriega as the following extract from a May 27, 1987 letter to Noriega from DEA head. John C. Lawn made abundantly clear:

> As you know, the recently concluded Operations Pisces was enormously successful, many millions of dollars and thousands of pounds of drugs have been taken from the drug traffickers and international money launderers. Your personal (emphasis added) commitment to Operations Pisces and competent professional and tireless efforts or other officials in the Republic of Panama were essential to the final positive outcome of this investigation. Drug traffickers around the world are on notice, that the proceeds and profits of their illegal ventures are not welcome in Panama.

INDEED!

In these last few lines we find the key to why the State Department turned on General Noriega and why a nationwide campaign of slander and libel was launched against the single most effective drug trafficking fighter in the world at the time. John C. Lawn's letters contrast very vividly with the sorry spectacle of Jose Blandon and convicted dope trafficker Milian's efforts to blacken the man most hated and feared by the Colombian dope barons, their Panamanian bankers and Eastern Liberal Establishment allies, in which lineup we include the *New York Times* and the *Washington Post*.

The Senate Subcommittee hearings rendered a terrible and unfortunate disservice to the American people by its support of the dope barons and their bankers, and virtually buried what was left of the lamentably weak war on drugs program, which President Reagan was supposed to have left in the hands of George H.W. Bush. All that remained of our tattered self-esteem as a nation opposed to the drug menace was Nancy Reagan's pathetic "Just Say No." Talk is indeed cheap, especially when compared with the brave acts of valor we can lay at the door of General Noriega and President Alan Garcia.

The U.S. establishment press, the jackals, who follow the dictates handed down by pack leader David Rockefeller were responsible for orchestrating the vicious anti-Noriega campaign in America, which led to the indictment by a Miami Grand Jury of the man so lavishly praised by the head of the DEA. Who is wrong here? Is it John C. Lawn? Is the Noriega he praised, really the same man portrayed as a friend and protector of narcotics traffickers by the cocaine mobster's press, its lawyers, its bankers, its paid liars and its policy making organizations?

At first glance there appears to be some confusion. Noriega is either clearly not the man John C. Lawn gave kudos to, or the Senate Subcommittee witnesses were liars. We leave it to you to draw your own conclusions. Let us return to the "enemies of Noriega" list and uncover the chief perpetrators of this most savage crime against the best opponent of dope traffickers in modern times.

General Ruben Darios Paredes

The retired former Commander of the Panama National Guard was General Noriega's most combative and dangerous enemy. In spite of the brutal cocaine mafia-style execution of his son, Paredes remained loyal to the Ochoa brothers, even after finding out that they lied to him when he phoned to enquire after his missing son. Paredes accepted the word of the Ochoas that his son was safe, even while the Colombian press was trumpeting the word that Rueben Jr. was already dead, the victim of "los grandes mafioses." Paredes had long-standing ties to Fidel Castro and his self-proclaimed "special friend" Colonel Roberto Diaz Herrera. Given these known facts, it is not surprising to find Paredes entertaining members of Carlos Ledher's private army of terrorists, the M19 at his home and shielding them after a unit of M19 was set up in Panama to protect the Darien cocaine laboratory and Israeli weapons caches.

Paredes was Kissinger, Linowitz and the State Department's choice to replace General Noriega once he was forced out by naked threats or Justice Department prosecutions. This was the basis of so-called "negotiations" with General Noriega that took place. In July 1987, Paredes threatened that war would break out in Panama if General Noriega did not resign. The role assigned to Paredes by Kissinger and Linowitz was that of a spoiler, to ensure that no individual and or political party became strong enough to threaten the vested interests of the dope barons and their banking nexus. As mentioned before, when Torrijos showed such signs, he met with a fatal plane "accident." Is there any real proof of the kind so avidly sought after by the Senate Subcommittee, and which it failed to find in the case of General Noriega, that could have linked Paredes to the cocaine barons and their dirty bankers? It is a matter of public record that the Ochoas lavished expensive gifts on Paredes, including costly thoroughbred walking horses, but that on its own is not enough evidence. Then there is the matter of the clearly established relations between Paredes's deputy, Lt. Colonel Julian Melo Barbua, whom we have already met, and whose close relationship with Ricardo Tribaldos, Jaime Castillo, Mendez and other Ochoa traffickers like Stephen Samos was not in dispute and which could in no wise have been concealed from General Paredes.

When Lopez Michelson met with the Colombian cocaine barons in Panama in 1984, it was Melo Borbua, who saw to it that they were not disturbed. I mentioned Stephen Samos, because he was married to Alma Robles, a sister of the Robles bothers whose law firm is used by the dope barons. Samos was a runner for the Fernandez syndicate-until he got himself caught. My information is that he was well known to Melo Borbua, and that his activities could not possibly have escaped the attention of a man like General Paredes.

Paredes, in spite of his known dope connections was much sought after by the jackals of the American media. He has received totally favorable press reviews, his seamy past apparently safely under wraps, in much the same way that General Pitovranov of U.S. Trade and Economic Mission (USTEC) is loved by the American press, notwithstanding his known past as head of a worldwide KGB kidnapping and murderer squad.

Dr. Norman Bailey

Bailey's past is tied up with the National Security Council where he served before joining up with Sol Linowitz of the infamous Panama Canal give-away. While a member of the National Security Council, Bailey was assigned to study the movement of narcotics money, which gave him first hand experience of Panama. As a direct result of his studies Bailey became friendly with Nicholas Ardito Barletta. Bailey was believed to have developed a hatred of Noriega, blaming him for Barletta's loss of his presidential job. Bailey is on record as saying:

> I began my war against Panama when my friend Nicky Barletta resigned as President of Panama.

Bailey learned a great deal about Panama's bank secrecy laws from the man responsible for making it a haven for drug traffickers and money laundering banks whose defender he now had become.

Why should Bailey have taken umbrage at the dismissal of Barletta? Because Barletta was the "man on the ground" representing British and American top-level Establishment figures, up to their eyebrows in the dope trade — from a safe distance of course. He was also the International Monetary Fund (IMF) man on the spot in Panama to see that its dictates were obeyed without question, and a favorite of George Shultz. When General Noriega resisted the IMF's austerity asset stripping packages, he came into head-on collision with Ardito Barletta, and vicariously, with the Washington elitist establishment. Unbeknown to

Bailey, General Noriega had been conferring with Alan Garcia, whose tactics had successfully defended Peru against IMF depredations, and which Noriega subsequently adopted for Panama.

As a result, Bailey was ousted when he tried to become the IMF's enforcer. At that point the decision to wage all-out war on Noriega and the National Guard was taken by George Shultz on the advice of Norman Bailey and his business partner, William Colby, whose company, Colby, Bailey, Werner and Associates had been consulted by the panic-stricken Panamanian and American drug money laundering bankers. From that moment onwards, General Noriega was never called anything other than "a dictator."

Bailey maintains that he was not interested in getting rid of Noriega. More importantly, he says, was getting rid of the militarily, because, according to Bailey, "Panama is the most heavily militarized country in the Western Hemisphere." This remarkable statement should be weighed against the known fact that it was Bailey who drafted the charges leveled against Noriega by Blandon, Eisenmann and Weedon. Bailey as a member of the civic action group that worked hard to oust Noriega and replace him with what Bailey liked to call a "Civilian Junta," that will hold free elections once it has gained power on which he sets a time limit of one year.

Bailey contributed heavily to the *New York Times* and *Washington Post* slander of Noriega, which he calls "98% fact." Even if only 2% is not fact, then surely his articles must be totally suspect? Through Bailey, the conspiracy against General Noriega turned the full circle from the cocaine barons in Colombia through to the elitists in Washington, London and New York. It was through Bailey that the connection was made between the low class murdering cocaine mafia and the untouchable respectable names in the social and political registers of Washington, Boston, London and New York epitomized by Elliott Richardson and George Shultz.

What is at stake is the massive amounts of cash generated by the as yet illegal narcotics traffickers which however, may not remain illegal for much longer, given the pressure on legislators to "ease up" on the "social use" of such drugs as marijuana and cocaine. Behind the pressure against cigarette smoking stood the dope lobby's campaign to legalize "light use" of dangerous habit-forming drugs. The Surgeon General says that nicotine is as habit forming as cocaine and heroin. The implications are obvious. Give up anti-social smoking with its proven cancer inducing risks, and switch instead to non-carcinogen cocaine or marijuana. Dope sales, which presently far outstrip the sales of gasoline, may soon also outstrip the sale of cigarettes.

The "market" for cocaine is as yet relatively untapped. If many more millions of people are turned into drug-dependant zombies, what of it, as Bertrand Russell would say if he were alive today. When Noriega was arrested by George Bush the elder and his army of 7,000 U.S. soldiers, the Soviet Union was the winner, through the partnership and Castro's Cuba. It was able to extend its influence across Latin America. A second benefit to the trade was the increased production of cocaine and marijuana it made possible. The U.S. felt the impact as drugs were now cheaper and greater quantities become available to "new" users, who may not necessarily become addicts, or so the rationale has it. In this, the drug barons were assured of the full support of the *New York Times* speaking on behalf of British interests and the *Washington Post*. Both newspapers have in past years published a number of articles in support of legalizing the use of marijuana and cocaine.

The Senate declared war on Panama just as it has declared war on South Africa. The patriotism of the American people was aroused by references to the military in Panama being a danger to insecurity of the Canal. De Concini was the worthless sop to the right wing who signed the give-away document, with "reservations," which were not agreed to by Panama, for which he was promoted as a wise and prudent man for demanding the codicil when it was, and is nothing but a bolt hole for the rats, who signed away the U.S. Canal at Panama. The situation in Central America became a danger to American national security interests. A Philippines style "democracy" was forced on Panama. In order to get the go-ahead on the Panama Canal Treaty, the Senate said General Noriega had to resign. If he refused to comply, he would be forced out. That was the consensus of the six-member Senate Staff Delegation, which visited Panama November 12-16, 1987.

The delegation made no mention of the frightful threat posed by the narcotics traffickers and their Cuba connection, not to mention the threat to our economy posed by the drain of U.S. dollars into Panamanian dirty money laundering banks. In the name of democracy, control of Panama was wrested from Noriega and handed to the international dope traders and Panama was turned upside down by the Canal Treaty. Not specifically spelled out, but clearly an implied threat, is the clear threat to send the U.S. military into Panama, if "disorders" threaten the safety of the Canal. It was to create such disorders that veteran troublemaker, John Maisto, was deployed in Panama.

John Maisto

Who is John Maisto? He was the number two man at the U.S. Embassy in Panama when the "transfer" to Panama was going on. Before that he was deployed to South Korea, the Philippines and Haiti to create unrest on the streets and to lead "demonstrations" against the authorities. He has been very active on the streets in Panama, and it is a disgrace that agent provocateur Maisto was allowed to get away with his scandalous behavior. The Senate willfully and with malice aforethought helped to create deteriorating conditions in Panama by continuing to insist that "dictator" Noriega was engaged in criminal activities and that his refusal to accept the U.S. defense rights, upon which the Panama Treaty is predicated, endangered the entire treaty.

"Defense rights" in this instance meant stationing American troops in areas where Maisto had been at work stirring up trouble, a deliberate provocation, as the military is fully aware of the inherent dangers in stationing troops in areas of civilian unrest. If it learned anything at all from Iraq, the military should know that it is wrong to put U.S. Military personnel in the middle of an untenable and volatile situation.

Another untruth that needs to be exposed is the story that General Noriega was receiving aid from Libya. This is a fabrication designed to discredit Noriega. My sources took three months to investigate the charges and found that they had no substance whatsoever.

The State Department had been running a disinformation campaign with the help of Ted Turner of CNN in much the same way as the BBC ran its disinformation campaign against the Shah of Iran. But in spite of all this, the bloodbath planned for Panama by the disinformation campaign and the scurrilous activities of John Maisto, failed to materialize. General Paredes, who as already explained, was the mouthpiece for the cocaine barons, their bankers and political backers, added his voice to the crescendo of calumny against General Noriega, predicting dire consequences for Panama if Noriega did not step down immediately. President Reagan, who hadn't the faintest idea of who the "bad guys" really were set an April 1988 deadline for Noriega to step down. As if Panama was a part of the U.S.!

When Noriega wouldn't oblige, the deadline was extended to mid-May. A Washington source said that Reagan wanted to have Noriega out of the way in time for his "summit" meeting with Gorbachev. Norman Bailey stepped up his demands that the Panama National Guard be disbanded as it represented a "danger" to the whole area.

Addressing a forum held at the George Washington University in Washington D.C., Bailey said that only if the people of Panama went out on the streets and got shot and beaten up would Noriega be budged. Unless the television cameras where on the spot to record such events, it would be a wasted effort. Nothing is going to happen in Panama, you are not going to get rid of Noriega and the institutions of the PDF if the people do not take to the streets, said Bailey. That is why Maisto was in Panama, where he put his mob-inciting experience gained in South Korea, the Philippines and Haiti, into practice.

What Maisto and Bailey wanted was a Panamanian "Sharpeville" — the State Department induced riot that swept the black township of Sharpeville in South Africa and resulted in 70 deaths among black rioters — which the cameras were conveniently on hand to record. Sharpeville has been a curse on South Africa ever since. The final straw supposed to break Noriega's back was the indictment handed down by a Miami Grand Jury. To summarize what had already taken place in Panama:

The drug forces and their bankers combined with the political establishment in Washington to get rid of General Noriega and replace him with a puppet regime directed from Washington. What were the reasons for this action? Firstly, Noriega was wrecking the lucrative, burgeoning cocaine and marijuana trade in Panama and secondly, he refused to co-operate with Kissinger's Andean Plan bent upon Central America becoming a Vietnam-style battleground for American forces.

These were considered as sufficient reasons to place Panama under siege conditions. What was the outcome? General Noriega refused to continue to step down. Contrived situations were then set in motion, including riotous assemblies, economic hardships and labor unrest, intended to make Panama ungovernable. At that point, the U.S. military stepped in, ostensibly to secure to the Canal, but in fact they were there to kidnap Noriega and shanghai him to Florida for trial. That is how U.S. foreign policy for Panama was conducted. Are we a nation fit to rule the West? I leave you to draw your own conclusions!

Was General Noriega in any way to blame for the unrest in Panama? Was he in any way, shape, or form, the drug-trafficker that the Grand Jury and the Senate alleged he was? Why was there so much attention paid to Panama all of a sudden; even greater attention than was paid to Panama at the time of the handing over of our Canal to "anti-

Communist" General Omar Torrijos?

When we hit someone in his or her pocketbook, we can be sure that it hurts. And that is exactly what General Noriega was guilty of doing. He hit the dope barons in their pockets. He cost the dirty dope money laundering banks a large slice of their ill- gotten profits. He brought the bankers into disrepute. He upset the status quo; he put teeth into Panama's bank laws. More than that, he got in Henry Kissinger's way and upset the Israeli arms sales in Central America. He tramped on the toes of powerful people. No wonder General Noriega was cast in the role of a villain. The Carter Presidency produced an explosion of cocaine trade. Within six months of Carter entering the White House, our currency situation was in disarray. The Federal Reserve had not anticipated the rush for dollars and it was hard put to meet the demand from Florida banks. The currency system was thrown into a disorderly pattern. Within six months of Jimmy Carter as President, Florida banks were turning over $514 billion in cocaine revenues.

Carlos Ledher of the Columbian drug cartel found a sympathetic and willing friend in Dr. Peter Bourne, Jimmy Carter's White House advisor on drugs. The Allman Brothers drug-sodden band was welcomed at the White House, notwithstanding the fact that they were "coke" users. Ledher cultivated his "Carter connection" and no doubt cheered when Bourne began issuing prescriptions for habit forming drugs for friends and colleagues ~ for which, incidentally, he escaped proper punishment.

Such "boom" conditions created a marvelous opportunity for the dope barons, especially in Panama. Torrijos did not care one way or the other about these happenings. To get control of the Canal Zone and build a viable Panamanian economy was what interested him the most. If cocaine and marijuana were a means to this end, then so be it! His attitude was "live and let live!"

The Carter administration backed IMF demands that Latin America grow "cash crops" (marijuana and cocaine) to meet their international debt obligations. The IMF officially encouraged several countries, including Jamaica and Guyana to grow "drug" cash crops. The IMF's position is on record. John Holdson, a senior official of the World Bank, stated that the coca industry is highly advantageous to producers, and added: "From their point of view they simply couldn't find a better product." The Colombian office of the IMF stated quite openly that as far as the IMF is concerned, marijuana and cocaine are just crops like any other crops that bring much needed foreign exchange into the economies of Latin American countries! It is not only the World Bank and the IMF that "approved" the drug trade.

The Midland and Marine Bank was taken over by the premier drug bank in the world, the Hong Kong and Shanghai Bank, with the express permission of former head of the Treasury Department, Paul Volcker, even though he knew full well that the purpose of the take-over was to permit the Hongshang Bank to gain a foothold in the lucrative cocaine-banking trade in Panama. In fact the acquisition of Midland by Hongshang was highly irregular, bordering close on a criminal act. The Midland Marine Bank was remarkable for one aspect; it operated as a clearing bank for Panama's dope banks!

So it was not just by coincidence that the Hong Kong and Shanghai Bank went after it! Nicolas Ardito Barletta was on the board of Midland Bank, as was Sol Linowitz. Funny how these names keep cropping up! Apparently Linowitz did not think it was a conflict of interest, when the time came to "negotiate" with Torrijos.

What about First Boston, up to its eyes in washing dirty dope money in conjunction with Credit Suisse? First Boston isn't just any bank. Its original owners were the old Eastern Liberal Establishment Perkins family, entwined with the White Weld Empire in Switzerland. Incidentally Perkins was the agent for J.P. Morgan and various other British houses operating inside the U.S. For the United States of America to go to such extraordinary lengths to get rid of a "dictator" of a small country ought to tell us something. It ought to make us curious to find out what lay behind the concerted effort by bankers, politicians and the jackals of the press to get General Noriega out of their way. It is my hope that with the information I have provided, you will now be able to understand why Panama is still under siege!

Since the first indication in 1986/87 that something had gone wrong with the drug banker's plans to use General Manuel Noriega as their tool, the Rockefeller and Wall Street banks began plotting to have him forced out of office. However, when all attempts failed, more drastic measures were investigated. Clearly by 1988, Noriega had become a serious impediment to the drug trade in Panama. The extraordinary lengths that Rockefeller went to in order to remove him because of his attacks on Ibero-American Bank of Panama, and the ensuing implications will now be examined.

Why was it necessary for President G.H.W. Bush to resort to a criminal action, to whit, an invasion of Panama and the kidnapping of its head of state? Many reasons for this truly lawless action have been advanced and we shall examine some of them. Had it not been that the American People were in a permanent fog, a huge outcry would have ensued over the invasion of Panama by the U.S. military.

Was Noriega in the employ of the Central Intelligence Agency? Did Alfredo Duncan, the DEA agent in charge in Panama believe this? If so, it might help to explain his weird conduct. According to reports from a deep cover DEA agent who has resigned from the service, he believed that Duncan had "an outstanding relationship with the CIA."

This was also the word around the Marriott Hotel in Panama; known by drug traffickers as "a DEA hotel." The same agent complained that he was never able to get Duncan "to do anything" about planned anti-drug operations in Panama in which his help was needed. When the order was given to arrest a man called Remberto, a kingpin in drug money laundering in Panama, Duncan apparently did nothing, and when questioned about his negligence, said that Remberto was spirited away by the CIA before he would take action.

Later it would be claimed that Remberto had ties to Noriega, but no evidence to substantiate the claim was ever produced. In 1986, Noriega closed down First Inter America Bank, when it was positively proved that it was owned by the Cali Cartel.

What was the Cali Cartel? It was probably one of the largest drug cartels in Colombia supposedly working with U.S. government agencies against the Medellin Cartel. The *Washington Post* admitted this. One of the official lobbyists for Cali was Michael Abbell, who was a Justice Department employee for 17 years. On October 28 and 29, 1989, President Bush and his allies held a summit meeting in

Costa Rica, which was attended by political leaders of Central and South America. At the press conference that followed, President Bush told reporters: "The days of that despot, the dictator (Noriega), are over."

This sent a signal to the press that the "urgent" matter of Noriega had now been resolved by joint consultation with Venezuela and Nicaragua, among others, although Bush officially tried to distance himself from President Daniel Ortega of Nicaragua. No matter how hard President Bush tried to give the appearance of a unanimous verdict against the Panamanian leader, the fact that the majority of the jury, Bolivia, Guatemala and the Dominican Republic didn't even show up for the "trial," a fact said to have infuriated Bush and his chief executive, James Baker III. President Carlos Salinas Gortari was supposed to have played a key role in the lynch mob affair. Perhaps Gortari decided that discretion was the better part of valor, having narrowly averted a major drug scandal in which one of his top generals was saved from being nabbed in a drug deal thanks to a timely warning phone call from then Attorney General Edwin Meese, of what was about to happen. Venezuela's President Carlos Andreas Perez, himself no knight in shining armor, was the one whom intelligence sources said there would be a coup against Noriega under cover of a "joint force" on October 3, 1989, but which attempt fizzled out. So did the attempt to pressure Latin American nations to break off diplomatic relations with Panama. President Bush told the heads of state that they had better get behind his plans for a confrontation with Noriega — or else. But the conference broke up without any definitive agreement being reached.

It speaks volumes of how much Bush feared Noriega and how low his government would stoop to gain its own ends.

Bush met with the Panamanian "opposition forces," the so-called Panamanian Democratic Opposition Civic Alliance, which consisted of public figures well known for having ties to banks in Panama and Florida that launder drug money. Its leader, Guillermo Endara went on television and all, but openly called for the assassination of Noriega.

On his return to Panama, Endara denied that he had ever called for such action. Noriega then countered the Costa Rica plotters by getting President Rodriguez to send an open letter to the Presidents of Latin America, which contained a copy of the offer made to the United Nations to make Panama the headquarters of a multinational anti-drug force, a fact President Bush had failed to bring out.

The October 3, 1989, letter to the U.N. called for such a force to be established by means of an international treaty that would guarantee it full authority in Panama, but there was no response from either the Bush administration or the U.N. The letter also scolded Venezuela and other "Bush partners" for calling for "democracy" in Panama, without ever mentioning the illegal and ugly boycott slapped in place by President Bush without good or valid reasons. All during October and November of 1989, U.S. forces in Panama kept up a running harassment of the Panamanian Defense Force, hoping to create an incident that would justify U.S. military intervention, but the PDF failed to oblige. It was later shown (May 1989), the Bush administration changed the rules of engagement for U.S. forces in Panama.

Henceforth the military was ordered to go out of its way to seek confrontations with the PDF. The Pentagon was secretly preparing to provoke Noriega's soldiers by running convoys through the outskirts of Panama City, which was in contravention with the treaty with Panama. The underlying premise was that Noriega would get angry and order the PDF to confront the U.S. convoys, thus setting the stage for a major U.S. intervention.

On July 8, 1989, General Cisneros, commander of the U.S. Army South in Panama, brushed aside attempts by the Organization of American States (OAS) to negotiate and settle the crisis. General Cisneros said that the OAS

> "...would not act firmly enough to dislodge Noriega. Speaking for myself, I believe this is the moment for a military intervention in Panama."

Since when does the U.S. military make political pronouncements? This action was by way of being a test case of what Bush had in mind for Iraq. On December 20, 1989, after all other methods had failed to dislodge the popular Noriega, Bush gave the green light for an act of violent aggression against the people of Panama resulting in the death of 7,000 Panamanians and the destruction of the entire area of Chorrillo through a sustained bombardment by U.S. troops and planes. This action, by the U.S. military, was an open act of aggression against a nation at peace, and was in gross contravention of the U.S. Constitution and The Hague and Geneva Conventions to which the U.S. is a signatory.

Let us examine the real reasons why President Bush, without first obtaining a declaration of war from Congress, went to war against the small nation of Panama, and in the manner of a desperado, ordered the kidnapping of the head of state? Why did President Bush have to resort to such desperate means to get rid of Noriega? Why did Bush resort to such gangster tactics? According to certain reports one of the major reasons was to warn Latin American nations that henceforth, if they failed to do the will of Washington, they too would face the threat of U.S. military action.

There is no reason to believe the massive propaganda campaign surrounding the illegal U.S. military action against Panama and Noriega, which the President would have the world believe would end drug trafficking in Panama, and which he had accused Noriega of running succeeded, even if only partially. There is no precedent in the U.S. Constitution or International Law that would have permitted an unprovoked attack on Panama.

What substantive proof did President Bush provide to back up his charges? Not a single shred of proof was ever offered. We were just supposed to take the President's word for it. What then were the objectives of the invasion? The first objective was to destroy the Panamanian Defense Force, the only force capable of keeping law and order in the country. With that objective reached, the next step was to install, by the most undemocratic means possible, a puppet regime consisting of persons with the closest ties to drug-money laundering banks, and known long-time supporters of the Bush family.

There was another, secondary, objective in destroying the PDF, and that involved the Panama Canal Treaties, under the terms of which the U.S. and Panama were to provide a joint defense of the Canal. This was to be phased out in 1999, by which time the PDF would be strong enough to take over the entire responsibility of policing the Canal and U.S. Military Forces would be obliged to depart the country. A key provision in the treaties stated that in the event that Panama did not live up to its obligations in providing such a security force, a "U.S. military presence shall be retained." This was thought to be a "good" provision when it was inserted by Sol Linowitz, who drew up the treaties. It was there to prevent any future Panamanian leader from "getting out of line," although no problems were envisaged with Omar Torrijos.

When Torrijos began reneging on his personal arrangements with David Rockefeller to protect the drug money laundering banks, it was not at that stage possible to destroy the PDF, although numerous attempts were made to get a revolt going that would divide the corps, all of which failed. Torrijos was therefore "liquidated" in the manner of the CIA. "Liquidation" became the language of the CIA following the tenure of Alan Dulles as its leader. Prior to that period, the word was never used by any U.S. intelligence agency. It was strictly a Stalin word.

Why should it be desirable to keep U.S. forces in Panama on a permanent basis? The advent of the Gulf War and the second invasion of Iraq by U.S. forces provides the key. The U.S. wanted to station a rapid deployment force in Panama to use against any recalcitrant Latin American and Caribbean nations, in the manner in which a rapid deployment force will be permanently stationed in Iraq to deal with Moslem countries that might wish they had never made friends with the U.S.

This is the so-called "hemispheric projection doctrine" established by Pentagon planners. We shall see similar permanent bases in many parts of the world, including Pakistan, South Korea, Somalia, Iran and Afghanistan as the United States eases into its role as the "big stick" enforcer for the global enforcer we have come to know as the New World Order. Yet thus far there has not been a single voice of protest raised against this in the Senate. I might add, without modesty, that these events were foretold in my book, *One World Order, Socialist Dictatorship.*[1]

Panama has become important as a base for U.S. operations against Latin American nations, who at some time in the future might rebel against the collector of tribute, the IMF, as they see their people and nations disappearing into the mire created by the international moneychangers. Clearly, immediate action would be required by the "international police force" of the IMF, the United States of America, in the event of any attempts by any country to kick out the IMF. Thus the bases at Fort Clayton have assumed a new importance. Latin America was intimidated and frightened by the ruthlessness of U.S. military actions in Panama. To be frank, the leaders of these nations did not expect it, and when it came, the ferocity scared them, which was exactly what it was supposed to do.

Evidently the majority of Latin American leaders believed that the Order of Skull and Bones was some sort of a benevolent organization, "like the Shriners" that would make for "a kinder, gentler America" as one official put it.

Little did they know of the involvement by the British Crown in U.S. affairs, nor of its long-standing connections to the drug trade. In support of the foregoing information came the offer by the forcibly, undemocratically installed Endara, that after the year 2000, all bases in Panama would be made available to the U.S. military.

---

[1] *One World Order Socialist Dictatorship*, John Coleman, Omnia Veritas Ltd, www.omnia-veritas.com.

The second objective of the Bush invasion of Panama was to install a new government of selected stooges with a history of long-standing alliances to banks, whose chief activities were to launder drug money for some of the most prominent cocaine cartels. In this Bush was commanded to protect the interests of the Rockefeller banks in Panama, which General Noriega had started to rip open and threaten to wreck. Indeed, this Bush objective was reached.

The third objective of the invasion of Panama was to represent to the American people that this was a major escalation of the President's war on drugs, that mythical, non-existent action which never gets anywhere. By invading Panama, Bush knew that his "drug war" would receive a big boost, especially on Capitol Hill, where lawmakers were becoming restive at the lack of progress and under constant pressure to legalize drugs. The next phase would be to mount a "war on terrorism," that would be global in reach and of open-ended duration.

By February 1990, some very strange things had begun to happen. The U.S. media, always a stalwart defender of Bush and his autocratic rule, began to make unfamiliar sounds. For instance, take the report contained in the New York Times of February 7. Even taking into account that the newspaper is an outpost of British Intelligence with U.S. managers at the helm, it nevertheless does not make any sense as to why the paper should have published the truth.

By referring to earlier articles it is remarkable how the *New York Times* (NYT) named the very people I was critical of for being too close to corrupt drug money laundering banks. Under the heading "Panama Is Resisting U.S. Pressure to Alter Inadequate Bank Laws," the article stated:

> An extensive review of Panamanian banking records and court documents shows that many senior leaders in the government (installed by the U.S.) while never accused of money laundering, have strong ties to corrupt banks. Several of the banks have either been indicted for money laundering or been shut down because of pressure from the United States.

The article did not say that it was action by Noriega, which had shut down these banks and that there has been no support from the U.S. for Noriega. Upon examining all the facts, the pieces of the puzzle began to fit its place. Of course the *New York Times* was trying to show that the U.S. had been the instigator of bank closures, when this was not the case at all, and moreover, by shifting the blame for "resistance" to changes allegedly emanating from Washington, it could be made to look as though the U.S. was really waging a drug war, but that the new government wasn't cooperating, which the reader must agree was quite a clever ploy.

The article went on to say:

> President Guillermo Endara has for years been a director of a Panamanian bank used extensively by Colombia's Medellin Cartel.

It was rewarding for me to get confirmation of the information given many years earlier in my monographs on Panama, even from such an unexpected source. Banco Interoceanico de Panama, one of two dozen Panamanian banks named by the FBI as drug money launderers, is the bank the New York Times was referring to. It then went on to say:

Mr. Endara was a corporate lawyer before becoming President, is a close friend of Carlos Eleta, a Panamanian businessman who was arrested in Atlanta in April (1989) on charges of conspiring to set up a major cocaine smuggling ring. Released on bail, he is now awaiting trial.

Of course the *New York Times* didn't go all the way, but what it did not say can be found herein, namely that it was not only Endara who was up to his hocks in the money-laundering banking business, but also his friends much favored by the Bush administration.

Other prominent members of the Bush administration's "Panama cabinet" include the following:

Rogelio Cruz

Cruz is Attorney General for Panama. He was formerly a director of the First Inter American Development Bank. This bank was owned by Gilberto Rodriguez Orejuela, a top man in the Cali Cartel in Colombia, which I have previously mentioned.

Guillermo Billy Ford

He is the Second Vice President and chairman of the banking commission. He also just happens to be the part owner of the Bank of Dadeland, which was specifically named in my monographs as a heavy drug money-laundering bank. The bank was also the clearinghouse for drug money for Gonzalo Mores, principle launderer for the Medellin cartel.

Ricardo Calderon

Calderon is the First Vice President of Panama, and records show that his family was heavily involved in suspect banks.

Mario Galindo

Galindo and his family, like Calderon, were involved with suspected drug money-laundering banks, one of which was the Banco del Istmos, whose chairman, Samuel Lews Galindo, was related to Mario Galindo.

All of the above were well known to Ivan Robles, who was employed at Dadeland Bank, and Antonio Fernandez who smuggled tons of marijuana into the U.S. In 1976, the Fernandez ring began to buy stock in the Dadeland Bank co-owned by Ford, Eisenmann and Rodriguez. President Bush warmly greeted Rodriguez as "porky" Endara's envoy to the United States. By establishing these men in leading roles in the Panamanian government, the Bush administration appeared to have succeeded in its second objective to make it easier, not harder for the drug trade to function in Panama, which as I said earlier, was the second objective of the invasion of Panama.

After calls that the secrecy laws of Panama be repealed, in defense of his position, Ford said that there was no need to change the law: "Secrecy will not be used for any illegal purposes." Others such as the Comptroller said that Panama wasn't going to change any laws.

> "We don't have to change our whole legal system because of drugs. We can't change our whole legal system because of one thing, drugs,"

said Ruben Diaro Carlos. Nobody dared mention that it was the very thing Noriega had been carrying out, and the main reason why he had to be forcibly removed.

On December 31, 1989, the prestigious Brazilian newspaper *Jornal do Brasil*, the country's biggest daily, featured a frontpage article under the heading "Dangerous Relations with Drug Traffickers," in which it mentioned the names of some of the members of the Bush "inner circle" government in Panama. These are the men who said before the verdict of the Noriega trial in Miami was in

"... if General Noriega is acquitted in Miami, they we charge him with murder."

I translated the article, which said in essence that Guillermo Endara would be especially vulnerable because of his connections with Carlos Eleta, "accused of laundering 600 kilos of cocaine and laundering drug money in the U.S." The article also mentioned the name of Vice President Calderon's brother, Jaime Calderon, who had ties to First Inter Americas Bank, owned by Gilberto Orejula, who was accused in 1985 of transferring $46 million, the proceeds of drug sales to the Banco Cafetero Panama branch in New York. The article said that Billy Ford was implicated with the Ambassador to Washington, Carlos Rodriguez, and Bobby Eisenmann in the laundering of drug funds through the Dadeland National Bank of Florida.

In a sub-heading, Guillermo Endara is described as "A Miserable Peon in the American's Game." The article said "Endara is called Pan Dulce (Sweetbreads), fat and soft." The article went on to say that Endara was one of the poor white oligarchy families, which have been on the scene since 1904:

> Endara began his political life as an obscure lawyer in Panama City in the law firm of Galileo Soliz, a foreign minister in one of the Anulfo Arias governments ... Endara never had his own ideas, he was a faithful as a puppy and repeated what Arias said, which is probably why Bush chose him to be his "yes man."

Were these the kind of men Bush wanted in control of Panama? Apparently so, yet while there is a great deal to point the finger of suspicion to the "Bush government" in Panama, not one single thing ever came up in court implicating Manuel Noriega. Wasn't this something a U.S. Grand Jury should have investigated a long time ago? Is this one of the reasons why Noriega was held incommunicado for so long? Was the Justice Department afraid of what Noriega may have told on the witness stand?

Developments in Panama show just how phony the Bush drug war really was. There are not too many people who do not believe this, and of course, it is the biggest plus that the proponents of legalizing drugs have going for them. Their attitude is "look, even the vast resources of the United States aren't enough to stop the drug trade.

Why try to fight the inevitable? Why not make laws that will centralize control and take drugs out of the hands of the criminal elements?" There are those lobbying Congress who threatened civil war if this was not done soon. The constant screening on nightly news of "police brutality" allegedly directed against mainly the poor in major U.S. cities is having the desired effect. We should not imagine that such reporting is "news." The aim and object of major network "news" during that period was to hammer home to the poor, that they are the victims of police brutality while the "big boys," usually whites, get away with it. Black leaders were demanding that either the "heat" be taken off the black population or else drugs be legalized.

The invasion of Panama gave the drugs lobby a leg to stand on. "If that hasn't stopped the flow of drugs, how are the police expected to cope," they asked. One of the pro drug-legalizer leaders, Andrew Weill, told a conference of the Drug Policy Foundation, that because of police brutality against urban blacks during drug raids, civil war could break out any time. The American Civil Liberties Union executive director Ira Glasser, told an audience that drug legalization has become a right wing issue, supported by such notables as George Schultz, William F. Buckley and Milton Friedman. Glasser urged that the nation "get beyond the negative and begin to win over police, legislators and the public" to the idea of legalized drugs.

Kevin Zeese, vice president and general counsel to the Drug Policy Foundation said:

> The drug war is more harmful than drugs are. That's pretty much what the balance comes down to. Is the drug war more dangerous to our society than the drugs are? Can we deal with the problem of drugs in a way less costly to our society- not just costly in economic terms, but in human terms as well?

Zeese went on to say that heroin was a way of escaping suffering, which although he did not advocate, he could understand. Now that kidnapped General Noriega is languishing in a federal prison in Miami, what does the Bush Justice Department intend to do with him?

One of the puzzling things I want to mention is the deafening silence from civil liberties organizations in this country and around the world as to the crimes committed against him by the U.S. government. One would imagine the kidnapping of a head of state would draw roars of protest from these watchdogs of liberty. Yet, no such thing has happened. Imagine what the result would have been if Nelson Mandela had been kidnapped in South Africa and taken to, let us say, Italy for trial. There would have been a never-ending clamor and uproar until Mandela was released. The kidnapping and illegal incarceration of Noriega points up the fact that we have a deplorable double standard in this country, one that seemingly, the American people do not think is all that bad or is it they have been brainwashed by the press?

Why was the trial of General Noriega delayed for so long? After all, every possible breach of his rights had already been committed, like monitoring phone conversations with his lawyer and freezing his funds so that he would be forced to accept a public defender. Also, with the U.S. in full and unfettered control in Panama, one would imagine that the Justice Department had the documentary evidence it needed to successfully prosecute him. Why the long, unseemly delay? Isn't justice delayed justice denied?

On November 16, 1990, Noriega made a statement to Judge William Hoevler, which is worth repeating, as it shows the extent to which justice was prostituted in the Noriega case:

> I am now at the mercy of a totally unfair, unjust system, which chooses my prosecutors, and now chooses my defense attorney. When I was brought to the United States, I mistakenly believed that I would be able to receive a fair trial. In order for this to come true, I also believed that I would be able to use my money to hire lawyers of my choice. It is painfully obvious that the United States

government does not wish me to be able to defend myself, and has done everything possible to deprive me of a fair trial and due process.

They have taken my money, deprived me of my lawyers, videotaped me in my cell, wire tapped my telephone conversations with my lawyers and even given them to the Endara government and to the press. The government of the United States has ignored my status as a prisoner of war and has violated the Geneva Convention.

Worst of all, they have not acted in a humanitarian manner. Despite repeated requests by the International Red Cross, they have violated my human rights by denying my wife and children visas to visit their husband and father and are a shameful violation of international law.

Obviously it is for the benefit of the United States government that I cannot defend myself, for what they fear I know. This is not a case about drugs. I realize that this case has implications to the highest levels of the United States government, including the White House.

I never had any illusions that this case was going to take place under equitable conditions, but I also never expected a virtual army of prosecutors and investigators on such an uneven field of battle and allowed only lawyers who receive no pay whatsoever and who are only permitted pistols while the prosecutor's office has nuclear weapons. They call this a fair fight; the battle 1 face ahead is very similar to when the United States invaded my country. That was one-sided and unfair, and so is this battle.

The situation in which Noriega found himself was the situation every American might one day be confronted by a corrupt and brutalized government. Noriega's plight made a mockery of the Fourth of July. It makes a mockery of the

United States Constitution. Meantime, there is not a single voice being heard in defense of Noriega, and to me, that is one of the most shameful things in a shameful situation. This is not a situation that can be ignored, for what happened to Noriega is the responsibility of every American. What has been largely ignored by the news media was the fact that by invading Panama and kidnapping General Noriega, the United States violated not only the U.S. Constitution, but also the Organization of American States (OAS) charter to which it is a signatory, particularly Articles 18, 15, 20 and 51.

Article 18 states:

> No state, or group of states has the right to intervene, directly or indirectly, for any reason whatever in the internal or external affairs of any other state.

Article 20 states:

> The territory of a state is inviolable; it may not be the object, even temporarily, of military occupation or other measures of force taken by another state.

Previously I referred to the matter of Bush not getting a declaration of war from Congress before invading Panama. Instead, Bush chose to sidestep the Constitution by informing Congress that he was invoking the National Emergencies Act, because of a state of national emergency caused by

> "an unusual and extraordinary threat to the national security and foreign policy of the U.S. posed by the Republic of Panama."

This so-called Act is a total farce, a "table raza," a worthless scrap of paper meant solely to subvert the U.S. Constitution.

The President lied to the American public when on December 20, 1989 he said:

> Last Friday General Noriega declared his military dictatorship to be in a state of war with the United States.

In fact, there was not a single piece of evidence to support such a preposterous charge.

In short, it was a blatant lie. Notwithstanding anything the President did or said, he failed to get a declaration of war against Panama, something he was to repeat in sending this nation to war against Iraq, and which will likely see the start of the death of the U.S. Constitution.

Another of the President's lies was his December 20 claim that

> "General Noriega's reckless threats and attacks upon Americans in Panama created an imminent danger to the 35,000 American citizens in Panama."

The truth is that there was only one attack on American servicemen, which arose out of the deliberate confrontation plan ordered by General Cisneros. This single tragedy came when three U.S. marines drove through three different PDF checkpoints. After being stopped at the fourth, there was an altercation between the PDF and the marines who were not in uniform.

The marines then drove off and after being repeatedly told to halt, shots were fired, one of which proved fatal.

President Bush is to blame for this soldier's death. On this single tragedy, Bush based his absurd claim that General Noriega had declared war on the U.S. and was "threatening the integrity of the Panama Canal Treaties." What Secretary Cheney told the American public was that the Bush administration had invasion plans ready as far back as March 1989.

Secretary Cheney himself tended to confirm this when he said on December 20:

> The order went out late on Sunday to implement the plan that had been in existence for some time. It was one of the first items I was briefed on when I became secretary of defense last spring.

Cheney was an inveterate troublemaker, a master of deception, and the United States is destined to loose a great deal of its treasure and its sons as a result of this man's duplicity. He should be barred from holding any future public office. Another administration lie was the announcement by Marlin Fitzwater, speaking on behalf of the President on December 20, 1989. Fitzwater told the nation that "the integrity of the Panama Canal Treaties is at risk." On the same date, James Baker III told the press that one of the objectives of the U.S. invasion was to "defend the integrity of the United States right's under the Article IV of the Panama Canal Treaties." But when asked to enumerate exactly what threats had been made by Noriega against the integrity of the treaties, Baker was unable to give even a single one. His response was:

> Well, that is very speculative other than — I mean, let me simply say with respect that that we have said before that we anticipated that there might be problems with respect

to the Canal if Noriega continued to retain power illegitimately. With respect to challenges to the integrity of our rights over the past two or three years, I would simply refer to the — over the past year or so — maybe I should back up, but, over the past year or so, I refer you to the continuing pattern of harassment that we've seen going on down there against Americans in the exercise of our treaty rights.

This fumbling, stumbling, bumbling and hastily concocted "proof," that Noriega had threatened US Canal rights was the best that Baker could come up with. What a sorry liar he turned out to be. Yet, on totally unsubstantiated, unsupported evidence, produced by President Bush, Secretary Cheney and Secretary Baker, this nation committed a grossly illegal invasion of a Sovereign State with which it had a treaty, and violated international and constitutional law.

By kidnapping General Noriega, our government descended to the level of Barbary Coast pirates, and in so doing, trampled the U.S. Constitution and International Law. Whether we like it or not, whether these words seem harsh and judgmental, the facts are the facts and cannot be denied. As a nation we are all equally responsible with President Bush for the lawless conduct of his administration, because we stood by and allowed it to happen without so much as a whimper of protest.

President Bush went on the air to tell Americans that one of the reasons why he ordered the invasion of Panama was "to defend democracy."

Although none of us realized it, this was to be one of the excuses for going to war against Iraq. Democracy had to be saved in Iraq, never mind that there never had been even a whiff of it in that dictatorship before. Besides, the U.S. is not a democracy, but a Republic. Nor are we the gendarmes of the world.

We are no longer a nation of laws since our war of genocide against Iraq! Democracy was alive and working in Panama. In spite of two years of gross, oftentimes crude and blatant interference in the internal affairs of Panama, in gross violation of the OAS Treaty to which the U.S. is a signatory, and in spite of at least two criminal attempts to murder General Noriega in May 1989, national elections were held.

What was the reaction of President Bush? Strongly supported by the jackals of the media, the Bush administration spent in excess of $11 million in backing the heavily drug-tainted opposition platform of Endara, Billy Ford and Calderon.

Drawing on the experience it had gained in the Philippine elections in which every branch of the U.S. government, including our intelligence services participated, Bush ordered the "Marcos Scenario" deployed against the people of Panama. The Bush-funded Endara gang set off a wave of unrest, stole the ballot boxes so that votes could not be counted, all the while loudly crying that votes had "been tampered with." It was an eerie replay of the Philippines election, complete with paid harlot "international observers" and the usual corps of media jackals, all howling their support of these falsehoods and an ominous portend of events to come in the U.S. itself.

In the midst of the Bush-created chaos and not being able to count the votes, the Panamanian government did what every other government would have, it annulled the elections. There was no other course it could have taken, given the massive and all-pervasive spoiler operations carried out by the Bush administration. In any case, that was what Bush hoped would happen. Even then, the Panamanian government was anxious to prove to the world that it was trying to do the right thing. It offered the opposition drug-tainted Endara gang the opportunity to participate in a coalition government.

On the advice of Washington, this generous offer was rejected by the "poor white peon" Endara. As we were to witness in the Iraqi "negotiations," Bush was hell-bent on the destruction of the PDF, the kidnapping of Noriega and the occupation of Panama, and no amount of goodwill offered by just men was going to be allowed to get in the way of his goals. Truly, under the Bush administration, America has become the most evil nation in the world, a veritable tyrant and a bully.

In one of the most astonishing and brazen acts of his career President Bush declared the drug-tainted Endara gang the "official government of Panama." These men, so heavily involved with drug laundering banks, were "sworn in" on a United States military base. If ever there was a law of the jungle, this was it. Then 45 minutes later the United States invaded the sovereign nation of Panama in one of the most blatant acts of aggression seen this century. If this was Democracy in action, then God help America, for what happened in Panama will surely be repeated domestically and indeed everywhere as the Republican Party becomes the Empire builder party.

We have let evil triumph by choosing to remain silent. We have been careless of the suffering of other nations at the hands of the U.S, so when our turn comes, we shall have only ourselves to blame. Our lack of protest, indeed our approval of the law of the jungle in action in Panama and in Iraq, makes us deserving of the punishment of Almighty God, which is surely going to fall on this nation because of our tolerance of evil deeds. Everywhere I travel I see posters and billboards: "God Bless America" and I have to ask myself why God would bless America when so much evil is being done in its name?

Another excuse for the invasion of Panama advanced by President Bush was that we were going into Panama "to combat drug trafficking." This is what Bush had the audacity to say on December 20, 1989, as he prepared his "Christmas Address" to the people of Panama and the U.S. An examination of the files of the DEA will quickly reveal that John Lawn, the former head of the DEA, had frequently cited in glowing terms the full cooperation he had received from General Noriega, the PDF and the Panamanian government. While General Noriega was in charge, the drug problem had distinctly abated.

On May 27, 1989, John Lawn wrote to Noriega congratulating him on the great help received in the successful seizing of drug runners' bank accounts, which Lawn called "the most successful undercover operation in federal law enforcement history."

Lawn stated as follows:

> Once again the United States DEA and the enforcement authorities of the Republic of Panama have joined efforts to strike an effective blow against drug traffickers...

Your personal commitment to OPERATION PISCES and

the competent professional and tireless efforts of other officials of the Republic of Panama were essential to the final positive outcome of this investigation.

Drug traffickers around the world are now on notice that the proceeds and profits of their illegal ventures are not welcome in Panama.

No wonder the lords and ladies of England and the pinstripe-suited denizens of the Wall Street banks began to worry. No wonder Rockefeller ordered Bush to get rid of Noriega and the Panamanian government post-haste. Noriega was really serious and in earnest about the war against drugs! Despite his statement that Noriega was a drug trafficker, President Bush never once offered one scintilla of proof to back up his claims.

In fact Adam Murphy, who was head of the Florida Task Force under the National Narcotics Border Interdiction System (NNBIS) stated categorically as follows:

> During my entire tenure at NNBIS and the South Florida Task Force, I never saw any intelligence suggesting that General Noriega was involved in the drug trade. In fact, we always held up Panama as the model in terms of cooperation with the U.S. in the war on drugs. Remember that a Grand Jury indictment in this country is not a conviction. If the Noriega case ever comes to trial, I will look at the evidence and that jury's findings, but until that happens, I have no first-hand evidence whatsoever of the general's involvement. My experience ran in the opposite direction.

Yet, notwithstanding the glowing recommendations in support of General Noriega and the Panamanian government made by John Lawn in his letter of May 27, 1987, less than one month later, Bush stage-managed a revolt against the lawful government of Panama. Carlos Eleta and his business partners, including Endara, the peon, immediately received the support of the U.S. military in Panama. We saw the very same modus operandi in Iran with sordid removal of Prime Minister Mossadegh at the investigation of U.S. General Hauser.

The disgusting breach of the OAS Treaty drew no protests from anyone in this country. Pat Robertson, the televangelist, and all his freedom loving associates stood mute in the face of provable lawlessness by the U.S. government. Therefore, we deserve what we are going to get when the government turns its lawless policies inwards and uses them internally on its citizens. It was the success of the Noriega Panamanian government in uprooting the drug mafia from Panama, conducted on the basis that it foolishly believed the United States was genuinely engaged in a war against drugs, and out of a genuine desire to fulfill their obligations to the U.S. in terms of the OAS Treaty, that was the undoing of the Panamanian government and General Noriega. By allowing President Bush to flout the U.S. Constitution, it will also be the undoing of the U.S., as we know it.

The "crime" of which Noriega and his government was guilty was that they did their job all too well, and in so doing, they stepped heavily on the toes of Dope International Limited and the lords, ladies and gentlemen who sit on its board. Let this be a lesson to anyone in the world who believes that the Bush administration is really engaged in a war on drugs. It is a phony war, no more and no less, and as several DEA deep cover field operators said, one of whom went after The Corporation, Bolivia's massive cocaine cartel and its Mexican partners, found to their cost, one was more likely to be "pensioned off rather than praised if one got too near to the top people in the drug trade, or suffer at the hands of a tyrant and have your fate settled by a kangaroo court.

The situation in Panama in 2009 is that drugs are flowing more freely than ever; and drug money laundering banks operate more freely. The economy of the country is in a shambles and awaits a U.S. injection of millions of U.S. dollars, but none of this really matters. What counts is that "democracy" triumphed in the country. Let this be a lesson to every Latin American Country! Let it be a lesson to every nation, that if this continues, no nation in the world will be safe. When you become a friend of the U.S. you may well loose your country.

Chapter Five

Pakistan's Role in the Drug War

The Muslim League formed Pakistan's first government under the leadership of Muhammad Ali Jinnah and Liaquat Ali Khan.

The Muslim League leadership of Pakistani politics decreased significantly with the rise of other political parties, including the Pakistan People's Party (PPP) in West Pakistan, and the Awami League in East Pakistan, which would ultimately lead to the creation of Bangladesh. The first Constitution of Pakistan was adopted in 1956, but was suspended in 1958 by Ayub Khan. The Constitution of 1973, suspended in 1977 by Zia-ul-Haq, was re- instated in 1991 and is the country's most important document, laying the foundations of government.

Pakistan is a federal democratic republic with Islam as the state religion. The semi-presidential system includes a bicameral legislature consisting of a 100-member Senate and a 342- member National Assembly.

The President is the Head of State and the Commander in Chief of the Armed Forces and is elected by an electoral college.

The Prime Minister is usually the leader of the largest party in the National Assembly. Each province has a similar system of government with a directly elected Provincial Assembly in which the leader of the largest party or alliance becomes Chief Minister. Provincial Governors are appointed by the President.

The Pakistani military has played an influential role in mainstream politics throughout Pakistan's history, with military Presidents ruling from 1958-71, 1977-88 and from 1999 onwards. The leftist PPP led by Zulfikar Ali Bhutto, emerged as a major political player during the 1970s. Under the military rule of Muhammad Zia-ul-Haq, Pakistan began a marked shift from the British-era secular politics and policies, to the adoption of Shariat and other laws based on Islam.

During the 1980s, the anti-feudal, pro-Muhajir Muttahida Qaumi Movement (MQM) was started by unorthodox and educated urban dwellers of Sindh and particularly Karachi. The 1990s were characterized by coalition politics dominated by the PPP and a rejuvenated Muslim League.

In the October 2002 general elections, the Pakistan Muslim League (PML-Q) won a plurality of National Assembly seats with the second-largest group being the Pakistan People's Party Parliamentarians (PPPP), a sub-party of the PPP. Zafarullah Khan Jamali of PML-Q emerged as Prime Minister, but resigned on 26 June 2004 and was replaced by PML-Q leader Chaudhry Shujaat Hussain as interim Prime Minister. On August 28, 2004, the National Assembly voted 191 to 151 to elect the Finance Minister and former Citibank Vice President Shaukat Aziz as Prime Minister. Muttahida Majlis-e-Amal, a coalition of Islamic religious parties, won elections in Northwest Frontier Province, and increased their representation in the National Assembly.

Pakistan is an active member of the United Nations (UN) and the Organisation of the Islamic Conference (OIC), the latter of which Pakistan has used as a forum for Enlightened Moderation, a plan to promote a renaissance and enlightenment in the Muslim world. Pakistan is also a member of the major regional organizations of the South Asian Association for Regional Cooperation (SAARC) and the Economic Cooperation Organization (ECO). In the past, Pakistan has had mixed relations with the United States especially in the early 1950s when Pakistan was the United States' "most allied ally in Asia" and a member of both the Central Treaty Organization (CENTO) and the Southeast Asia Treaty Organization (SEATO).

During the Soviet-Afghan War in the 1980s Pakistan was a crucial U.S. ally, but relations soured in the 1990s, when sanctions were applied by the U.S. over suspicions of Pakistan's nuclear activities. The September 11 attacks and the subsequent War on Terrorism have seen an improvement in U.S.-Pakistan ties, especially after Pakistan ended its support of the Taliban regime in Kabul. This was evidenced by a drastic increase in American military aid, which saw Pakistan take in $4 billion more in three years after the 9/11 attacks than in the three years before.

Pakistan has long had troubled relations with neighboring India. The dispute over Kashmir resulted in full-fledged wars in 1947 and 1965. Civil war in 1971 flared into the simultaneous Bangladesh War of Independence and the Indo-Pakistani War of 1971. Pakistan conducted nuclear weapon tests in 1998 to counterbalance India's nuclear explosion test called "Smiling Buddha" in 1974 and Pokhran-II in 1998 respectively and became the only Muslim nuclear weapons state. Relations with India steadily improved following peace initiatives in 2002.

Pakistan maintains close economic, military and political relationships with the People's Republic of China.

Pakistan also faces instability in the Federally Administered Tribal Areas, where some tribal leaders support the Taliban. Pakistan has had to deploy the army in these regions to suppress the local unrest, in Waziristan. The Waziristan conflict ended with a recently declared peace agreement between the tribal leaders and the Pakistani government that is expected to bring back stability to the region. Additionally, the country has long faced instability in Balochistan, its largest province by size, but smallest by population.

The army was deployed to fight a serious insurgency within the province from 1973-76. Social stability resumed after Rahimuddin Khan was appointed martial law administrator beginning in 1977. After relative peace throughout the 1980s and 1990s, some influential Baloch tribal leaders restarted a separatist movement when Pervez Musharraf took over in 1999. In an August 2006 incident, Nawab Akbar Bugti, the leader of the Baloch insurgency, was killed by Pakistani military forces. On November 3, 2007, President Musharraf declared an emergency rule across Pakistan and purported to suspend the Constitution, imposing martial law.

In Islamabad, troops apparently entered the Supreme Court and were surrounding the judges' homes and opposition leaders like Benazir Bhutto, Imran Khan were put on house arrest. Justice Abdul Hameed Dogar has been appointed as the new chief justice of Pakistan, due to the refusal of the Iftikhar Muhammad Chaudhry to endorse the emergency order, declaring it unconstitutional, though he himself took oath under PCO in 1999. In response, Pakistan was suspended from the councils of the Commonwealth of Nations on November 22, 2007.

In recent years, militant Islamists in the Tehreek-e-Nafaz-e — Shariat-e-Mohammadi (TNSM) organization, led by radical cleric Maulana Fazlullah have rebelled against the Pakistani government in Swat in the North-West Frontier Province. In 59 villages, the militants had set up a "parallel government" with Islamic courts imposing sharia law.

After a four-month truce ended in late September, 2007, fighting resumed. The paramilitary Frontier Constabulary had been deployed to the area to quell the violence, but seemed ineffective.

Militants were reported on November 16, 2007, to have captured Alpuri district headquarters in neighboring Shangla. The local police fled without resisting the advancing militant force which, in addition to local militants, also included Uzbek, Tajik and Chechen volunteers.

To roll back militancy and restore order, the Government of Pakistan deployed a force from the regular Pakistani Army which was successful in retaking the lost territory, sending the Islamists into their mountain hide-outs, but attacks by suicide bombers on the Army continued.

It was reported that the United States Special Operations Command was considering alternatives to render effective aid to Pakistan with respect to this and other al-Qaeda related insurgencies in the tribal areas of Pakistan, but prospects remain uncertain, even after a special study done in 2008.

The late Benazir Bhutto was the first woman elected to lead a post-colonial Muslim state. She was twice elected Prime Minister of Pakistan. She was sworn in for the first time in 1988, but removed from office 20 months later under orders of then President Ghulam Ishaq Khan on grounds of alleged corruption.

In 1993 Bhutto was re-elected, but was again removed in 1996 on similar charges. Bhutto went into self-imposed exile in Dubai in 1998, where she remained until she returned to Pakistan on October 18, 2007, after General Musharraf had a special law passed absolving her from all corruption charges by which she was granted amnesty and all corruption charges were withdrawn. The eldest child of former premier Zulfikar Ali Bhutto — a Pakistani of Sindhi extraction — and Begum ("Lady") Nusrat Bhutto, a Pakistani of Iranian-Kurdish extraction, she has been accused by her niece Fatima Bhutto of gross corruption and of having been responsible, along with her husband Asif Zardari, for the assassination of her brother Murtaza Bhutto in 1996.

After two years of schooling at the Rawalpindi Presentation Convent, Bhutto was sent to the Jesus and Mary Convent at Murree. She passed her A-level examination at the age of 15, the usual age being 17. After completing her early education in Pakistan, she attended Harvard University, where she obtained a B.A. degree cum laude in comparative government.

The next phase of her education took place in the United Kingdom. Between 1973 and 1977 Bhutto studied Philosophy, Politics, and Economics at Lady Margaret Hall, Oxford. She completed a course in International Law and Diplomacy while at Oxford. In December 1976 she was elected president of the Oxford Union, becoming the first Asian woman to head the prestigious debating society. On 18 December 1987 she married Asif Ali Zardari in Karachi. The marriage produced three children. Benazir Bhutto's father, former Prime Minister Zulfikar Ali Bhutto, was dismissed as Prime Minister in 1975, on corruption charges similar to those Benazir Bhutto would later face.

In a 1977 trial on charges of conspiracy to murder the father of dissident politician Ahmed Raza Kasuri, Zulfikar Ali Bhutto was sentenced to death. Despite the accusation being "widely doubted by the public," and despite many clemency appeals from foreign leaders, including the Pope, Bhutto was hanged on April 4, 1979. Appeals for clemency were dismissed by then President General Muhammad Zia-ul-Haq. Benazir Bhutto and her mother were held in a "police camp" until the end of May, following her father's execution.

In 1980, her brother Shahnawaz was killed under suspicious circumstances in France. The killing of another of her brothers, Mir Murtaza in 1996, contributed to destabilizing her second term as Prime Minister. Bhutto, who had returned to Pakistan after completing her studies, found herself placed under house arrest in the wake of her father's imprisonment and subsequent execution. Having been allowed in 1984 to return to Britain, she became a leader in exile of the PPP, her father's party, though she was unable to make her political presence felt in Pakistan until after the death of General Muhammad Zia-ul-Haq. She had succeeded her mother as leader of the Pakistan People's Party and the pro-democracy opposition to the Zia-ul-Haq regime.

On November 16, 1988, in the first open election in more

than a decade, Benazir's PPP won the largest bloc of seats in the National Assembly. Bhutto was sworn in as Prime Minister of a coalition government on December 2, 1998, becoming at age 35 the youngest person — and the first woman — to head the government of a Muslim majority state in modern times.

But her government was dismissed in 1990 following charges of corruption, for which she never was tried. Zia's protege Nawaz Sharif subsequently came to power. Bhutto was re-elected in 1993, but was dismissed three years later amid a chorus of corruption scandals by then president Farooq Leghari, who used the Eighth Amendment discretionary powers to dissolve her government. The Supreme Court upheld President Leghari's dismissal with a 6-1 ruling.

In 2006, Interpol issued a request for the arrest of Benazir and her husband. The criticism against Benazir came largely from the Punjabi elites and powerful landlord families who opposed Bhutto as she pushed Pakistan into nationalist reform, over the interests of the feudal lords, whom she blamed for the destabilization of her country. After being dismissed by the president of Pakistan on charges of corruption, her party lost the October elections. She served as leader of the opposition while Nawaz Sharif became Prime Minister for the next three years. Elections were held again in October 1993 and her PPP coalition was victorious, returning Bhutto to office. In 1996 her government was once again dismissed on corruption charges.

French, Polish, Spanish and Swiss documents led to further charges of corruption against Benazar and her husband, and both faced a number of legal proceedings, including a charge of laundering money through Swiss banks. Her husband, Asif Ali Zardari, spent eight years in prison on similar corruption charges. Zardari, released from jail in 2004, has suggested that his time in prison involved torture.

A 1998 *New York Times* investigative report indicates that Pakistani authorities had documents that uncovered a network of bank accounts, all linked to the family's lawyer in Switzerland, with Asif Zardari as the principal shareholder. According to the article, documents released by the French authorities indicated that Zardari offered exclusive rights to Dassault, a French aircraft manufacturer, to replace Pakistan's aging air force fighter jets in exchange for a 5% commission to be paid to a Swiss corporation controlled by Zardari. The article also said a Dubai company received an exclusive license to import gold into Pakistan for which Asif Zardari received payments of more than $10 million into his Dubai-based Citibank accounts. The owner of the company denied that he had made payments to Zardari and claims the documents are forgeries.

Bhutto maintains that the charges leveled against her and her husband are purely political. "Most of those documents are fabricated," she said, "and the stories that have been spun around them are absolutely wrong." The Auditor General of Pakistan (AGP) report supported Bhutto's claim. It presented information suggesting that Benazir Bhutto was ousted from power in 1990 as a result of a witch hunt approved by then- president Ghulam Ishaq Khan. The AGP report said Khan made unlawful payments of 28 million Rupees to file 19 corruption cases against Bhutto and her husband in years 1990-1993.

The assets held by Bhutto and her husband were duly

scrutinized by prosecutors who then alleged that the Bhuttos' Swiss bank accounts held $840 million. Zardari also bought a neo-Tudor mansion and estate worth over £4 million in Surrey, England, U.K. The Pakistani investigators tied other overseas properties to Zardari's family. These included a $2.5 million manor in Normandy owned by Zardari's parents, who had modest assets at the time of his marriage. Bhutto denied holding substantive overseas assets.

Bhutto and her husband, until recently, continued to face wide-ranging charges of official corruption in connection with hundreds of millions of dollars of "commissions" on government contracts and tenders. But because of a power-sharing deal brokered in October 2007 between Bhutto and Musharraf, Benazir and her husband were granted amnesty. If that stands, the development could trigger a number of Swiss banks to "unlock" accounts that were frozen in the late 1990s. The executive order could in principle be challenged by the judiciary, although the judiciary's future is uncertain due to the same recent developments. On July 23, 1998, the Swiss Government handed over documents to the government of Pakistan which related to corruption allegations against Benazir Bhutto and her husband. The documents included a formal charge of money laundering by Swiss authorities against Zardari.

The Pakistani government had been conducting a wide-ranging inquiry to account for more than $13.7 million frozen by Swiss authorities in 1997 that was allegedly stashed in banks by Bhutto and her husband. The Pakistani government recently filed criminal charges against Bhutto in an effort to track down an estimated $1.5 billion she and her husband are alleged to have received in a variety of criminal enterprises. The documents suggest that the money

Zardari is alleged to have laundered was accessible to Benazir Bhutto and had been used to buy a diamond necklace for over $175,000.

The PPP responded by flatly denying the charges, suggesting that Swiss authorities have been misled by false evidence provided by Islamabad. On August 6, 2003, Swiss magistrates found Benazir and her husband guilty of money laundering. They were given six-month suspended jail terms, fined $50,000 each and were ordered to pay $11 million to the Pakistani government.

The six-year trial concluded that Benazir and Zardari deposited in Swiss accounts $10 million given to them by a Swiss company in exchange for a contract in Pakistan. The couple said they would appeal. The Pakistani investigators say Zardari opened a Citibank account in Geneva in 1995 through which they say he passed some $40 million of the $100 million he received in payoffs from foreign companies doing business in Pakistan.

In October 2007, Daniel Zappelli, chief prosecutor of the Canton of Geneva, said he received the conclusions of a money laundering investigation against former Pakistani Prime Minister Benazir Bhutto on Monday, but it was unclear whether there would be any further legal action against her in Switzerland:

> The Polish Government has given Pakistan 500 pages of documentation relating to corruption allegations against Benazir Bhutto and her husband. These charges are in regard to the purchase of 8,000 tractors in a 1997 deal. According to Pakistani officials, the Polish papers contain details of illegal commissions paid by the tractor company in return for agreeing to their contract. It is alleged that the

arrangement "skimmed" Rs 103 million rupees ($2 million) in kickbacks.

The documentary evidence received from Poland confirms the scheme of kickbacks laid out by Asif Zardari and Benazir Bhutto in the name of (the) launching of Awami tractor scheme.

Benazir Bhutto and Asif Ali Zardari allegedly received a 7.15 percent commission on these purchase through their front men, Jens Schlegelmilch and Didier Plantin of Dargal S.A., who also received about $1,969 million for supplying 5,900 Ursus Tractors.

In the largest single payment investigators have discovered, a gold bullion dealer in the Middle East is alleged to have deposited at least $10 million into one of Zardari's accounts after the Bhutto government gave him a monopoly on gold imports that sustained Pakistan's jewelry industry and drug trade. The money was allegedly deposited into Zardari's Citibank account in Dubai. Pakistan's Arabian Sea coast, stretching from Karachi to the border with Iran, has long been a gold smugglers' haven.

Until the beginning of Bhutto's second term, the trade, running into hundreds of millions of dollars a year, was unregulated, with slivers of gold called biscuits, and larger weights in bullion, carried on planes and boats that travel between the Persian Gulf and the largely unguarded Pakistani coast. The desolate Maccra coast is also the dropping off point of huge shipments of heroin and opium out of Afghanistan and is the mainstay of the gold trade with the British Bank of the Middle East based at Dubai.

Shortly after Bhutto returned as prime minister in 1993, a

Pakistani bullion trader in Dubai, Abdul Razzak Yaqub, proposed a deal. In return for the exclusive right to import gold, Razzak would help the government regulate the trade. In November 1994, Pakistan's Commerce Ministry wrote to Razzak informing him that he had been granted a license that made him, for at least the next two years, Pakistan's sole authorized gold importer.

In an interview in his office in Dubai, Razzak acknowledged that he had used the license to import more than $500 million in gold into Pakistan, and that he had traveled to Islamabad several times to meet with Bhutto and Zardari. But he denied that there had been any corruption or secret deals. "I have not paid a single cent to Zardari," he said.

Razzak claims that someone in Pakistan who wished to destroy his reputation had contrived to have his company wrongly identified as the depositor. "Somebody in the bank has cooperated with my enemies to make false documents," he said.

At no time was the enormous heroin and opium trade mentioned although it is the basis for gold trades at Dubai. The peasant opium poppy growers of Helmand in Afghanistan do not take paper money for their crops, and are always paid in gold. Since September 2004, Bhutto lived in Dubai, United Arab Emirates, where she cared for her children and her mother, who is suffering from Alzheimer's disease, traveling to give lectures and keeping in touch with the Pakistan People's Party supporters. This naturally raises the question. Why Dubai?

The answer is obvious. Bhutto stayed in Dubai to oversee

the huge gold trades conducted through the Bank of Dubai. She and her three children were reunited with her husband and the father in December 2004 after more than five years.

On January 27, 2007, she was invited by the United States to speak to President Bush and congressional and State Department officials. Bhutto appeared as a panelist on the BBC TV program Question Time in the U.K. in March 2007. She has also appeared on BBC current affairs program News Night on several occasions. She rebuffed comments made by Muhammad Ijaz-ul- Haq in May 2007 regarding the knighthood of Salman Rushdie, citing that he was calling for the assassination of foreign citizens.

Bhutto had declared her intention to return to Pakistan in 2007, which she did, in spite of Musharraf's statements of May 2007 about not allowing her to return ahead of the country's general election, due late 2007 or early 2008, because she might be assassinated. Yet other sources warned her of a very strong possibility that attempts would be made to assassinate her. The drug trade is a very dangerous business, and those who make the mistake of crossing the king-pin families in this lucrative trade, run a great risk.

U.S. historian Arthur Herman, in a controversial letter published in the *Wall Street Journal* on June 14, 2007, in response to an article by Bhutto, highly critical of the president and his policies, described her as "...One of the most incompetent leaders in the history of South Asia," and asserted that she and other elites in Pakistan hated Musharraf because he is a muhajir, the son of one of millions of Indian Muslims who fled to Pakistan during partition in 1947. Herman also claimed:

"Although it was muhajirs who agitated for the creation of Pakistan in the first place, many native Pakistanis view them with contempt and treat them as third-class citizens."

Nonetheless, as of mid-2007, the U.S. appeared to be pushing for a deal in which Musharraf would remain as president, but step down as military head, and either Bhutto or one of her nominees would become prime minister.

Through all of its internal strife, the drug trade continued on its way, seemingly oblivious to the ongoing political strife. No one was bold enough to step forward and block the route from Afghanistan to the coats of Maccra that would have interdicted the massive opium trade. There was just too much at stake for any one to attempt such a monumental task. In 2007, the DEA declared that opium from Afghanistan had reached a record production of 6,000 tons for the year, notwithstanding that the main growing area of opium poppy, Helmand, was constantly patrolled mainly by British and American troops under NATO command.

The drug overlords have shown the world once again, that no matter what sort of government controlled a country (any country except Russia) they can continue to do business using innovative methods, a change of pace and direction. I doubt very much whether the new U.S. President, Barack Obama, will be allowed to implement steps that he may wish to put into action. Time will tell. In the meantime the multi-billion dollar business keeps on rolling along. The Drug Cartel's new "business plan" includes switching the distribution of cocaine from Mexico, the Caribbean and Panama, to far-distant Africa.

In addition, the managers have slashed the price of cocaine

50 percent at the wholesale level, making the cost of a "line" of cocaine less than $5.00, within easy reach of all customers at the street level. The beauty of this plan from the Cartel's position is that African import countries are easy to manage, and with one or two notable exceptions, law enforcement is extremely lax, and highly susceptible to bribery.

Another country of entry for cocaine into the European market is "Kosova," the brainchild of Richard Holbrook, the so-called architect of the destruction of Serbia, which was simply given as a free gift to the decadent white slave and drug trafficking Albania. Yes, believe it or not, Albania's Gross National Product is made up of revenues derived from drug trafficking and white slave trafficking.

Henceforth, the cocaine trade will flourish in Kosova as it has done for a hundred years in Albania. Any attempts by DEA agents to stop it will be met with intimidation and murder of its agents. Until the U.N. anti-narcotics agency and the anti-drug forces of Western Europe and the United States can get a handle on the new distribution routes, the Drug Cartel barons are going to have a virtually clear run.

An Update April 2009

Three years ago, the Mexican authorities, urged on by the U.S., declared war on the drug dealers. Because of that action, Mexico is facing a rapid decline and collapse, unless the U.S. steps up to the plate and helps Mexico with troops and adequate funding. While the new Obama administration's Secretary of State acknowledges that the battle raging in Mexico poses a very real danger if it spills over into the U.S., she recently told CBS news that she was preparing to take steps to help Mexico with men and money. In the face of the known fact that the Mexican Drug Lords are terrorizing Mexico with acts of brutality that are horrifying — the hitherto reluctance on the part of the U.S. to come to its aid is hard to understand. It is not as if Mexico is far removed from the U.S., or that we do not have close relations. In fact, we are closer to Mexico diplomatically speaking, than we are to Canada.

In January 2009, Mexican drug terrorists kidnapped 10 soldiers. A short while thereafter, their bodies, riddled with bullets, were dumped along the side of a busy road. In another instance, a citizen thought to be a police informant was abducted, his head cut off, and his body hung over the side of a road bridge in full view of thousands of motorists using the underpass.

In 2008, 6300 people were kidnapped and killed by the drug terrorists. In fact, Mexico City has earned the unenviable reputation of being the kidnap capital of the world. Rich and poor alike are victimized. Recently 250,000 people gathered in the main square of Mexico City to protest the slow government response to the drug lords. But the truth is that Mexico does not have the manpower or the money to mount the kind of overwhelming response to the drug barons that is needed. And another thing, the drug terrorists are better-armed than the Mexican Police and Federal Drug Agents. The drug traffickers have fully automatic rifles and hand grenades and have regularly out-gunned the Mexican police in a number of pitched battles. Their superior weapons are purchased for cash from dealers in the United States. The U.S. government says it is pushing to close down these gun sales. A recent U.N. survey of Mexico reports that its drug trade amounts to a staggering $38 billion a year, with more and more traffickers getting into the business every month. Corruption among the Mexican anti-drug forces is rife and although the Attorney General of Mexico says that he has adopted new measures to curb the drug trade, everything points to a rise in violent drug-related crime. There are some bright spots in the dark picture:

In 2008 Mexico arrested 57,000 drug traffickers and it has just been disclosed that the U.S. government has committed an additional $56 million a year to help Mexico in its struggle against the drug barons. As feared, the Mexican drug terror has spilled over into 230 U.S. cities, and is today in mid-April 2009, the number one crime in America. It is our duty to join in the struggle now going on against the dangerous menace of drug trafficking threatening America. We must realize that we are at war with ruthless men who are determined to undermine and bring down our great Republic. The U.S. must follow the example of President Betancourt of Colombia. The entire future of our nation is at stake. This is not a war from which we can stand aside It is a fight to the death. We must win this war. If we do not, then the enemy within our gates will have taken a giant step forward in implementing its program of slavery and darkness for us all, as envisioned in the plans of the One World Government.

Other titles

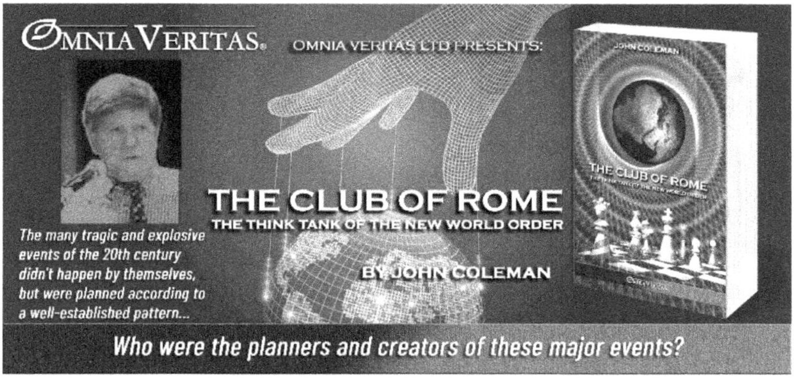

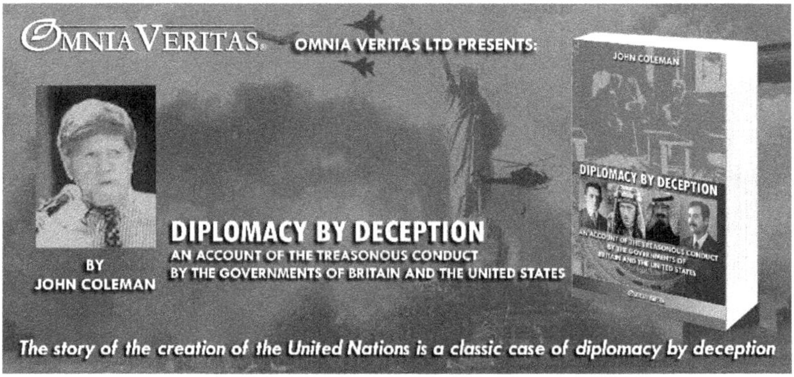

OMNIA VERITAS OMNIA VERITAS LTD PRESENTS:

ABORTION
GENOCIDE IN AMERICA

BY JOHN COLEMAN

I MAINTAIN THAT WHEN A WOMAN AGREES TO AN ABORTION IN A NON-LIFE THREATENING SITUATION, SHE HAS TAKEN LEAVE OF HER SENSES AND SHOULD BE ADJUDGED "TEMPORARILY INSANE."

ABORTION SHOULD BE EXPLAINED AS EUPHEMISM FOR "MURDER BY DECEPTION"

OMNIA VERITAS OMNIA VERITAS LTD PRESENTS:

FREEMASONRY
from A to Z
by John Coleman

In the 21st century, Freemasonry has become less a secret society than a "society of secrets".

This book explains what masonry is

OMNIA VERITAS OMNIA VERITAS LTD PRESENTS:

THE ROTHSCHILD DYNASTY

by John Coleman

Historical events are often caused by a "hidden hand"...

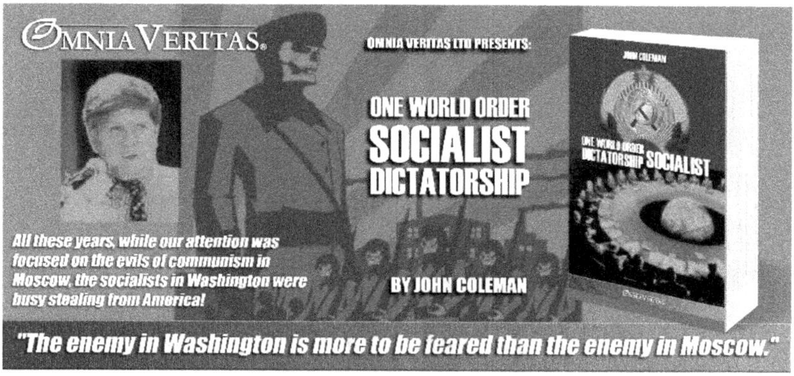
OMNIA VERITAS
OMNIA VERITAS LTD PRESENTS:
ONE WORLD ORDER
SOCIALIST
DICTATORSHIP
All these years, while our attention was focused on the evils of communism in Moscow, the socialists in Washington were busy stealing from America!
BY JOHN COLEMAN
"The enemy in Washington is more to be feared than the enemy in Moscow."

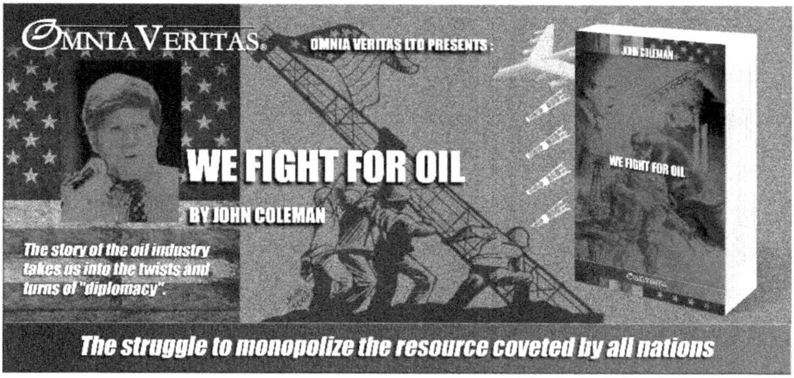
OMNIA VERITAS
OMNIA VERITAS LTD PRESENTS:
WE FIGHT FOR OIL
BY JOHN COLEMAN
The story of the oil industry takes us into the twists and turns of "diplomacy".
The struggle to monopolize the resource coveted by all nations

OMNIA VERITAS
Omnia Veritas Ltd presents:
THE SVALI CHRONICLES
BREAKING FREE FROM MIND CONTROL
TESTIMONY OF AN EX-ILLUMINATI
The Illuminati are a group of people who follow a philosophy known as "illuminism" or "enlightenment".
Understanding the programming of the Illuminati sect

Omnia Veritas Ltd presents:

HERVÉ RYSSEN

PLANETARIAN HOPES

The triumph of democracy over communism seemed to have opened the door to a new era, to a "New World Order", and to prepare all nations for an inevitable planetary merger.

The idea of a world without borders and of a finally unified humanity is certainly not new...

Omnia Veritas Ltd presents:

HERVÉ RYSSEN

PSYCHOANALYSIS of JUDAISM

Judaism, in fact, is not only a religion. It is also a political project whose aim is to achieve the abolition of borders, the unification of the earth and the establishment of a world of "peace".

This book represents the most comprehensive study of the Jewish question ever undertaken.

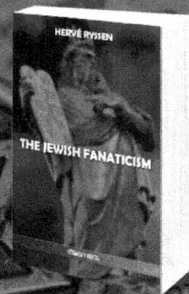

Omnia Veritas Ltd presents:

HERVÉ RYSSEN

THE JEWISH FANATICISM

The resulting dissolution of national identity protects them from a possible nationalist backlash against the power they gained, especially in finance, politics and the media.

The Jewish people promote a project for the whole of humanity...

The "Jewish mafia", that one, does not exist; the Western media do not talk about it...

The cynicism and malice of these conspirators is something beyond the imagination of most Americans.

Only one people bas irritated its host nations in every part of the civilized world

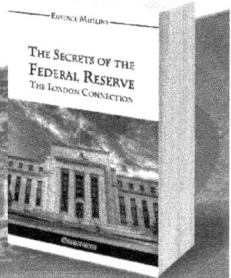

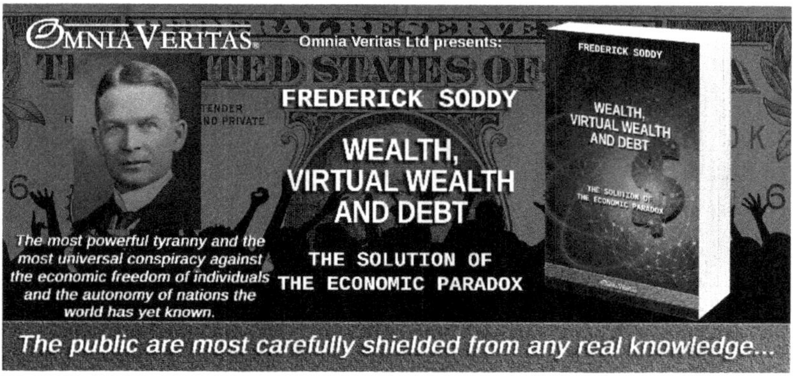

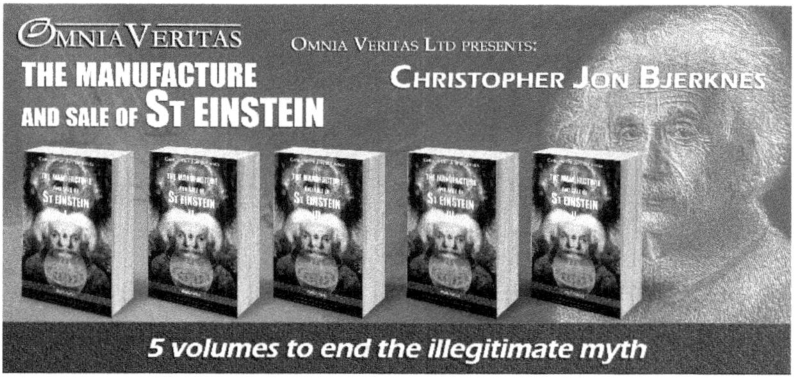

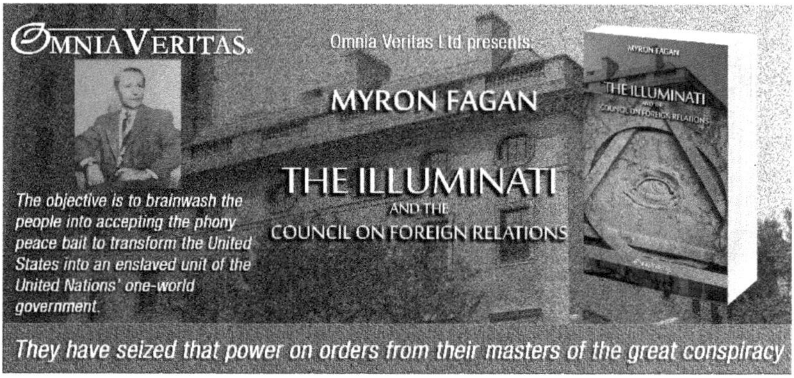

www.ingramcontent.com/pod-product-compliance
Lightning Source LLC
Chambersburg PA
CBHW070905270326
41927CB00011B/2461